Praise for

MAKE YOUR MARK

"Brad Gray has a remarkable gift for merging the best tools we use to interpret the Bible today. Here he employs historical geography, the culture of ancient Israel, Hebrew language insights, and a wide knowledge of the Bible to bring to life the stories of Samson that are frequently neglected in the church. His aim is not mere exposition, however. His heartfelt desire is to see these ancient inspired stories find new life for believers and he does it with enthusiasm, humor, and skill. MAKE YOUR MARK is as fascinating as it is inspiring. And particularly for those Christians who may think they've heard it all in the Bible, Brad Gray proves that there are fantastic surprises still to be discovered."

—Gary M. Burge, PhD, professor of
New Testament at Wheaton College and
Graduate School

"Samson is the perfect archetype for the conflicted superheroes we find in movies today. Despite his supreme strength, he's often hardly heroic in how he fulfills God's calling. What can we learn from his weaknesses? By digging into Samson's life in its ancient context, Brad Gray has excavated much fresh insight for today. I was delighted and convicted by Brad's thoughtful heart, his humor, and his passion for studying God's Word in its original time and place."

—Lois Tverberg, author of *Sitting at the Feet of Rabbi Jesus* and *Walking in the Dust of Rabbi Jesus*

"Brad Gray's mighty fine book MAKE YOUR MARK probably should be titled "It Will Leave a Mark" because it will! Over the years, I have had the unspeakable pleasure of teaching preaching to literally hundreds of young men and women all eager to take their place in the long line of preachers who have gone before them. I keep in my mind a list of the "best of the best" I have ever taught, and Brad Gray is on that list. He may actually be at the very top of that list in this particular regard; he is the most relentless studier of the text I have ever taught. He tirelessly turns over every stone in sight to see what is just beneath the surface! What a wonderful gift to once be a teacher of a person who then becomes your teacher! If you read MAKE YOUR MARK like I did, it will leave a mark on you, and you will be better for it!"

—Dr. Timothy Brown, president and Henry Bast professor of Preaching, Western Theological Seminary, Holland, Michigan

"MAKE YOUR MARK brings three dimensional insights to a mysterious story. The image of Samson has long been that of a muscular one man wrecking crew. By guiding us through the geography, customs, and language, Brad Gray provides a refreshing look at an enigmatic character. In the process, he motivates us to become better stewards of our own calling, gifts, and opportunity."

—Jeff Manion, senior teaching pastor, Ada Bible Church, and author of *The Land Between* and *Satisfied*

"Brad Gray provides a rare combination of cultural understanding, geographical context, historical perspective, and biblical insight, making this book a powerful read. The life lessons from Samson's story are clear and highly relevant for today's culture."

—Kirk Cousins, NFL quarterback and author of *Game Changer*

"In MAKE YOUR MARK, Brad Gray helps strip away our western cultural assumptions and gives us a fresh look into the story of Samson. Along the way he gives us practical and biblical instruction that helps us navigate through our own stories as we become a part of the larger story."

—TobyMac, Grammy award–winning artist, producer, songwriter, and author of *City on Our Knees*

MAKE YOUR MARK

GETTING RIGHT WHAT SAMSON GOT WRONG

BRAD GRAY

Faith Words

NEW YORK ■ BOSTON ■ NASHVILLE

Hachette Book Group
1290 Avenue of the Americas,
New York, NY 10104

Visit our website at www.faithwords.com
Printed in the United States of America
First Edition: August 2014
10 9 8 7 6 5 4

The FaithWords name and logo are trademarks of Hachette Book Group, Inc.

The publisher is not responsible for websites (or their content) that are not owned by the publisher.

Library of Congress Cataloging-in-Publication Data

Gray, Brad.
    Make your mark : getting right what Samson got wrong / Brad Gray. — First edition.
        pages cm
    Includes bibliographical references.
    ISBN 978-1-4555-7360-8 (trade pbk.) — ISBN 978-1-4555-7359-2 (ebook)
1. Samson (Biblical judge)   I. Title.
    BS580.S15G73 2014
    222'.32092—dc23
                                                                    2013044014

To my wife, Shallon…

An ezer kenegdo *par excellence, and the greatest woman I've ever met. Thank you for your endless love, encouragement, and challenge.*

Contents

MAKE
YOUR
MARK

CHAPTER 1

Under the Sea

When my family and I lived in Israel, we often planned weekend getaways. If I had a weekend off from my studies in Jerusalem, we'd rent a car and head off to explore new hikes, visit new sites, or revisit our favorite places. (I've lost track of how many times we visited the Galilee area—Jesus knew how to pick a place!) We were in Israel for a limited time and wanted to make the most of every opportunity. We'd return exhausted, but we had the time of our lives, and we loved every minute of it.

One particular weekend in 2009, our getaway was strictly for the purpose of rest and relaxation. I had a few days off from my studies and my brain needed a rest. I've never enjoyed education as much as while studying in Israel, but even the good things in life need a siesta. So we rented a car and headed off to our destination.

For months we'd wanted to visit the city of Eilat. Nestled in the southernmost reaches of Israel, adjacent to Egypt and Jordan, and within eyeshot of Saudi Arabia to the southeast, Eilat sits on the northern tip of the Red Sea. It's a popular destination for both international and domestic tourism, and a city renowned for its nightlife, impeccable climate, and beaches. Since we were visiting for the purpose of rest and relaxation, it was the beaches that drew our greatest interest.

We arrived at the beach late morning on a picturesque day. It was seventy-five degrees with a light breeze. We found an empty area with a couple of beach chairs and settled into our joy. With the cool sand cascading between our toes, we gazed upon a deep and vibrant blue sky and watched the white, puffy clouds meander across the heavens. Could life be any better? This was paradise. We were experiencing the best Eilat had to offer.

Or were we?

Because then it happened.

I'm sure it had been going on for some time, but we were so entranced in our solitude, we hadn't even noticed. People started walking out of the sea. Lots of them, like they'd just ascended some underwater stairway. And all of them were ranting and raving about something. Their faces were lit up with excitement as they gestured wildly to one another. It didn't take us long to make the connection that their amazement had something to do with the masks, snorkels, and fins they all possessed.

Clearly we hadn't gotten the memo. Something spectacular was going on and we were missing out. My look of perplexity and curiosity caught the attention of an amused bystander, who approached and informed us we could rent snorkel gear in the shop we'd recently passed through to enter the beach.

Within minutes, we had fins on our feet, masks on our faces, snorkels in our mouths, and a whole lot of anticipation. Once underwater, we understood. Less than a hundred feet from shore was one of the most exquisite coral reefs we'd ever seen. And with exquisite coral reefs come exotic fish. The experience left us breathless.

A whole new world lay under the sea—a world deep and meaningful and full of new surprises. It was a world we didn't know existed while lounging on the beach less than a hundred feet away, and yet it was there all along. All we needed was someone to guide us in the right direction and provide the necessary gear.

Many stories in the Bible function in a similar fashion. We've read them time and again, but our view has been from the beach, and we've been oblivious to the reality that there's more under the sea. But once we descend the depths, we recognize these stories are deeper and more meaningful than what we've come to understand or believe.

Take the story of Samson.

When you hear the word "Samson," what immediately comes to mind?

Perhaps it's his superhuman strength capable of performing enormous feats, such as tying three hundred jackals tail-to-tail or collapsing the pillar supports of a temple, killing thousands of Philistines. Or the infamous cat-and-mouse game he plays with an enticing woman named Delilah. Maybe it's his ability to end lives as he shreds a lion with his bare hands or strikes down a thousand Philistines with a fresh jawbone (can't forget about the "fresh" part—nobody wants to be killing anyone with a "dry" jawbone). Or maybe it's that Samson was a great military hero who led the Israelites in the precarious time of the Judges. From the beach, this story has an impressive view.

But perhaps the story isn't beckoning us to see it from the beach, but from under the sea. Maybe our perspective has been limited, and the story is pleading with us to get under the water and see it anew. If so, then you may wonder how we know we've been viewing the story from the beach, and not from under the sea.

Let's grab a mask and take a preliminary look.

The Samson narrative begins in Judges 13, and as the curtain is lifted, we are immediately ushered into a devastating reality.

Samson's mother (whose name we aren't given) is unable to conceive. For a woman in the ancient world, you couldn't find a more demoralizing or painful predicament.

The two most important aspects of life for the ancients were land and family. To be exiled from your land or to be unable to pass along your family heritage through the birth of children was far worse than any other tragedy, including death. Furthermore, in an honor and shame culture, in which every activity of life brought either honor or shame, infertility was the pinnacle of shame for a woman. This is why in Genesis, Jacob's wife Rachel, during her stage of barrenness, bitterly proclaims to her husband, "Give me children, or I'll die!" (Gen. 30:1). This despairing situation for Samson's mother is no different. For Manoah's wife, as Samson's mother is called, this is a gut-wrenching reality.

However, the fact she is barren tips us off to an unfolding pattern. In addition to Manoah's wife, there are six other women in the biblical narrative who experience a period of barrenness. Perhaps you're familiar with some of these names: Sarah, Rebekah, Rachel, Hannah, the Shunnamite's wife, and Elizabeth.

Three of these women are Matriarchs (Sarah, Rebekah, and Rachel) who give birth to such figures as Isaac, Jacob, and Joseph. Hannah is the mother of Samuel, who becomes a pivotal leader and linchpin between the Judges and the Monarchy. And Elizabeth is the mother of John the Baptist, who will lay the foundation for the coming of Jesus.

Not a bad cast of mothers and sons.

Now what can be observed is that in every case of barrenness in the Bible, God shows up and provides a way for the woman to conceive,[1] and the boys of these formerly barren women grow up to become very important figures in the history of the Israelite people.[2]

So when we read that Manoah's wife is barren, we are deeply saddened at her predicament, but we recognize her barrenness is a harbinger of something epic to come. God is up to something, and so our anticipation builds. This is a moment of colossal significance, and we are not disappointed by what ensues.

Samson's Nazirite Calling

An angel of the LORD appears to Manoah's wife, announces she will have a child, and specifically states he is to be a "Nazirite" from birth. Manoah is not present at this monumental conversation, and therefore his wife recounts the event, again highlighting the fact the child is to be a "Nazirite." What's fascinating is that this Nazirite stipulation is so critical to the conversation that it has to be mentioned twice in this opening chapter![3]

For Samson to be identified as a "Nazirite" would've meant adherence to the parameters of the Nazirite vow found in Numbers 6. It's a vow of complete dedication to God, and one that both men and women could enter into. Interestingly enough, while Numbers 6 indicates the vow is voluntary and for whatever length the individual desires, Samson's vow is involuntary and without end. God specifically called Samson to be a Nazirite for life.

Prior to this point in the biblical story, there is no indication of anyone being a Nazirite for life, let alone specifically commanded by God to do so. Samson's Nazirite calling is unprecedented.

Only Samuel and John the Baptist will become Nazirites for life in the remaining pages of the Scriptures,[4] and Samuel's will be a result of a voluntary vow made by his mother, Hannah. Furthermore, in the cases of both Samuel and John the Baptist, the Nazirite status is alluded to with references to restrictions of the Nazirite vow.

Only with Samson is the specified term, "Nazirite," used. It's as if God is making it undeniably clear this Nazirite identity is to be of paramount importance in the life of Samson.

Numbers 6 lists three restrictions a Nazirite must adhere to. First, a Nazirite must not consume anything from the grapevine, including wine, or any other alcoholic drink. Therefore, no grapes and definitively no wine. Second, a Nazirite must not cut their hair. Their long hair is the visible identifier of the vow taken before God. And third, a Nazirite is not allowed to be in the vicinity of a dead body.

Wait a minute.

Did you catch that last restriction?

A Nazirite is not allowed to be in the vicinity of a dead body.

Which means a Nazirite is not allowed to kill.

Therefore, Samson is not allowed to kill.

Uh-oh, we're no longer on the beach.

But hold on, that doesn't make any sense. Samson's gift is unparalleled human strength, and much of the Samson story entails him utilizing this strength to rid the earth of those oppressive Philistines, whom he has been commissioned to deal with. What's more, God seems to be blessing his efforts. But if Samson is commanded by God to be a Nazirite, which invariably comes with the stipulation of not killing, why then would God give Samson superhuman strength if he's not allowed to kill? It doesn't make any sense.

That is, it doesn't make any sense if the story is operating under the sea and we've been viewing it from the beach.

Hence, this book.

I believe many of us have only seen and heard the Samson story from the beach, and yet there's a world under the sea waiting to be explored. It is a world that provides a deeper and more meaningful understanding of the story. And it is a world that has been there all along; we just haven't had the guidance and gear to get there.

However, this journey isn't simply for the purpose of better understanding the story. We don't want it to simply remain a story. We want it to do something to us—to inform us, challenge us, direct us, and most important, transform us.

I believe some of the most foundational truths and struggles of life are seen implicitly and explicitly in this story of Samson. This isn't a story about muscles and testosterone, nor is it simply for men. It is a story for humanity because it is a story about humanity.

It is a story about calling and the use of our gifts.

It is a story about successes and failures.

It is a story about forgiveness and revenge.

It is a story about hope and despair.

It is a story about light and darkness.

It is a story riddled with anger, pride, arrogance, lust, selfishness, and a host of other human emotions we all deal with from time to time.

Essentially, it is a story about life.

And so it beckons us to grab a mask, a snorkel, and a pair of fins and dive in—to leave what is known on the beach and enter the unknown under the sea.[5] But even more than that, it beckons us to anticipate that once we've surfaced after all we've seen and experienced, we will do so as people who've been profoundly challenged and changed.

CHAPTER 2

Rushed by the Spirit

We shuffled into the classroom. The early risers were raring to go. The night owls were wondering how they got stuck taking an 8 a.m. class, and why the college didn't have a later offering. I often wondered if the professors despised these early morning classes as much as their students. Knowing half of your students are comatose until at least ten must be quite a challenge when you're teaching on a subject you've dedicated your life's work to. But then again, it pushes you to find creative ways to get your points to stick. On this particular day, our professor did just that.

Positioned front and center was a television. After dispensing a few pleasantries to begin the class, the professor walked over to the television and began showing a scene from a movie. I hadn't seen the movie before so I watched carefully, trying to discern the purpose for which it was being shown. After six or seven minutes, the professor jumped to another scene that preceded the one we'd just seen. Three minutes later he did it again. Only this time the scene was near the end of the movie. Five minutes later, the professor again skipped to another part of the movie. Unable to determine where this scene fell, we watched as before, with a bit of confusion. Four minutes later, we were taken to another scene. After viewing it for less than a minute, the professor quickly rose from his chair, shut off the television, and asked, "So what's the story about?"

After a prolonged silence, we began taking stabs at identifying the overall narrative. One by one, our responses were met with, "Nope, try again." After nearly ten minutes of hopeless guessing, our professor smiled slowly. Drawing out every last millisecond of his dramatic pause, he leaned forward into our confused silence and said, "You can't understand the parts until you've understood the whole."

Brilliant.

The same rings true for the Samson story. Samson's life spans four chapters (Judges 13–16), roughly the length of the New Testament book of Ephesians, and is the longest narrative in the book of Judges, covering a period of twenty years and beginning sometime around 1100 BC. It's a nonstop, action-packed, tension-filled story, replete with numerous twists and turns. There's never a dull moment, and our main character is complex. It's a story that possesses all the elements of cinematic drama we've come to appreciate. And if we're going to understand it anew, we have to first understand how all the pieces fit together to shape the whole.

So allow me to guide us through the story. As I do so, there will be times where I'll dive deeply into the story and expound upon its colorful details. At other times, I'll hover closer to the surface because we'll be doubling back to these areas and going deeper in subsequent chapters. And since we've explored the key elements leading up to Samson's birth in Chapter 1, we'll pick up the narrative flow at the end of Judges 13.

Setting the Stage

The end of Judges 13 does what any great story does early in its telling. It introduces the main character, provides the setting, and gives the inciting incident that spins the story into motion. Notice how the narrator has succinctly conveyed these elements:

> The woman gave birth to a boy and named him Samson. He grew and the LORD blessed him, and the Spirit of the LORD began to stir him while he was in Mahaneh Dan, between Zorah and Eshtaol. (vv. 24–25)

Following the elaborate introduction of the angel visiting Manoah and his wife, and the angel providing the details surrounding the life of their unborn son, Manoah's wife gives birth to our main character. It is here we learn he is given the name "Samson."

Names in the ancient world are significant. It was understood that one's name contained the essence of the person's identity, and also his or her destiny. Names were chosen with care. People didn't just choose a name because it was popular or because it rolled off the tongue nicely. You chose a name based on what you hoped your child would become, and then spent the remainder of your life praying your child would live into the identity of the name.

After considerable thought and prayer, Manoah and his wife choose the name "Samson"—at least that's how it gets rendered in English. In Hebrew his name is *Shimshon*, which means "of the sun/light" or "little sun/light."[1] It may seem like an odd name, but it's loaded with meaning. In the ancient world, the sun or light was always connected to a god. For example, in Egyptian culture, the highly esteemed sun god was Re. There was no sun god in Hebrew culture. The Israelites upheld a monotheistic belief in an almighty creator God who made the sun, and was therefore not the sun. However, the sun, and by connection, light, became metaphors for God. [2] Figuratively speaking, God was the great light.

Based on their context, it's safe to assume the reason Samson's family gives him this name is because he is to be a reflection of God. [3] As a Nazirite called to live out the ways of God, Samson was to be like the great light. As the "little light," he was to point people toward the "greater light" (God).

The setting is between Zorah and Eshtaol at Mahaneh Dan ("the encampment of Dan"), where part of the tribe of Dan has settled. This area sits just to the north of the eastern end of the Sorek Valley, roughly fifteen miles west of Jerusalem (as the crow flies). *Sorek* is a Hebrew word meaning "vine." It makes you wonder if Samson, a Nazirite who must stay away from the vine, found it ironic living in the vicinity of "Vine Valley."

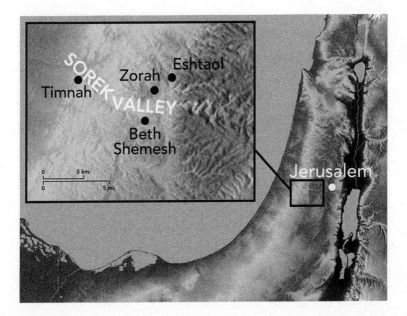

The Sorek Valley was a strategic location at the northern end of a geographical region known as the Shephelah. Often translated as "lowland" or "foothills,"[4] the Shephelah served as a buffer zone between the flat plain on Israel's western coast and the high hill country where significant cities such as Gibeah, Jerusalem, and Hebron were located. Politically, the Shephelah also served as a buffer zone between the Israelites and the Philistines, for at this time in Israel's history the Philistines had taken up residence on the coastal plain, with their five main cities (known as the "Philistine Pentapolis") dominating the landscape. As one of six valleys that served as corridors between the coastal plain on the west and the hill country on the east, the Sorek Valley was highly coveted by both the Israelites and the Philistines. To live in the Shephelah was to live in the tension between these two worlds.

So we've got our main character and our setting, and now we need our inciting incident. Interestingly enough, it is the Spirit of the LORD who spins this story into motion. Again, as the narrator tells it, "and the Spirit of the LORD began to stir him while he was in Mahaneh Dan, between Zorah and Eshtaol" (Judg. 13:25).

When you read or hear the word "stir," it may conjure up the idea of being motivated or empowered—as if the Spirit of the LORD is motivating or empowering Samson in this moment. However, that doesn't capture the essence of this rare Hebrew verb, used only five times in the Old Testament. The word translated as "stir" is the Hebrew verb *pa'am*, which means "to disturb, thrust, or push."[5] Meaning, the Spirit of the LORD has to give him a swift kick in the loincloth to get him moving. Which tells us there's some reluctance on Samson's part to begin living into the identity and calling he's been given from God. But there's movement. Our story has been kicked into motion, and we wonder how Samson will live out his calling in a difficult region.

Getting Married

Samson's first action is visiting a city by the name of Timnah. Timnah is located in the central region of the Sorek Valley, six miles west of Zorah and Eshtaol. Owing to the flatness and ease of travel within the valley, the walk would've taken Samson only a couple of hours. Although only a short distance away, Timnah was much different than Samson's stomping grounds. Evidence from the archaeological excavations suggests Timnah was "a well-fortified, densely populated, urban center"[6] belonging to the Philistines, Israel's arch nemesis. Its name—Timnah—means "forbidding," which lends itself well to the unfriendly nature it possessed. Samson doesn't seem to care.

After returning home from his adventure, he tells his parents of a Philistine woman he saw, and with unabashed boldness, he demands they get her as his wife. Taken aback by this brazen request, Samson's parents offer their rebuttal. Their plea falls on deaf ears. Manoah and his wife cave, knowing full well this flies in the face of not only God's commands, but their community's social customs as well.

After bullying his parents into submission, Samson heads back down to Timnah, parents in tow. Along the way, something unexpected occurs.

As they approached the vineyards of Timnah, suddenly a young lion came roaring toward him. The Spirit of the LORD came powerfully upon him so that he tore the lion apart with his bare hands as he might have torn a young goat. But he told neither his father nor his mother what he had done. (Judges 14:5–6)

Now that's impressive. The vast majority of humanity would have soiled their loincloths. Samson, on the other hand, rips the beast to shreds. There's a tension, however, in what we've just read. Remember, a Nazirite isn't allowed to kill. This goes for both humans and animals. So irrespective of the circumstances, in this moment Samson breaks the Nazirite vow. What makes the scene even more confusing is the presence of the Spirit of the LORD. Why does God seem to empower Samson to break the vow He had given him to keep?

What's more, we're left wondering why Samson doesn't tell his parents what happened after they reunite in the city (apparently Samson and his parents separated for a bit on the walk to Timnah, reflected in the fact his parents don't witness this event) or on their way home from Timnah. It appears Samson's aware he's broken his Nazirite vow. According to the regulations outlined in Numbers 6, if a Nazirite's hair becomes defiled by being in the presence of a corpse, they must go immediately to the tabernacle (which is currently in Shiloh, a seventy-mile round trip from Timnah) and undergo an eight-day restoration process, which includes shaving one's head, along with offering a sin, burnt, and guilt offering.[7] The last thing Samson wants is to spend the time and money required for his restoration. That would totally cramp his style.

After an unspecified period of time, Samson heads back to Timnah with his parents for the wedding. Along the way, we're told Samson "turned aside to look at the lion's carcass, and in it he saw a swarm of bees and some honey. He scooped out the honey with his hands and ate as he went along. When he rejoined his parents, he gave them some, and they too ate it. But he did not tell them that he had taken the honey from the lion's carcass" (Judg. 14:8–9).

And once again, Samson breaks his vow. Although not explicitly stated in the Numbers 6 list of restrictions, a Nazirite, like any Israelite, wasn't allowed to eat anything unclean.[8] Lions are unclean animals. They are not kosher. Technically speaking, bees are also unclean, but the honey they produce is not. So there's nothing wrong with Samson eating honey in general. The issue is this honey has been in contact with the decaying carcass of an unclean animal.[9] What's more, Samson causes his parents to become defiled because he doesn't tell them the origin of the honey, and they consume it. So not only is Samson blatantly disregarding God's instructions, but he is causing his parents to unknowingly live in disobedience to God.

The downward spiral continues. Samson arrives in Timnah for the marriage ceremony and accordingly "held a feast, as was customary for young men" (Judg. 14:10). The word "feast" is the Hebrew word *mishteh*, which means "drinking bout."[10] One of the restrictions of the Nazirite vow is not consuming any kind of alcohol. Thus, Samson breaks the vow again.

Undeterred and certainly unconcerned, Samson lives fully into the seven-day wedding celebration customary for the day, and while doing so offers a riddle to have some fun with the locals. A successful answer entails Samson providing his thirty groomsmen each with a set of clothes. An unsuccessful answer requires the thirty men to each give Samson a set of clothes.

After three days of unsuccessfully solving the riddle, the unfriendly Philistine folks present an ultimatum to Samson's wife (one of their own, let me remind you), "Coax your husband into explaining the riddle for us, or we will burn you and your father's household to death. Did you invite us here to steal our property?" (Judg. 14:15). Samson has deeply offended these men and shamed them in front of their family and friends—something one doesn't *ever* do in an honor and shame culture.

Recognizing her life is on the line, Samson's wife pleads with him in tears until he reveals the answer—seven days later! She passes along the answer and Samson loses the bet. He demonstrates his displeasure by remarking, "If you had not plowed with my heifer, you would not have solved my riddle" (Judg. 14:18). And in case you're wondering, yes, this statement is as derogatory in Hebrew as it is in English. Nothing like being called a cow at your reception by your husband.

What comes next is perplexing. We are told, "Then the Spirit of the LORD came powerfully upon him. He went down to Ashkelon, struck down thirty of their men, stripped them of everything and gave their clothes to those who had explained the riddle. Burning with anger, he returned to his father's home" (Judg. 14:19).

First, let's acknowledge the obvious. Samson kills thirty men, and breaks the vow. Again. Second, let's also acknowledge once again the Spirit of the LORD shows up prior to him killing. It's problematic, but for the time being, let's sit in this tension. What I'm most interested in at this moment is the implications and perplexity of where he does his killing—Ashkelon. This is where a map is helpful.

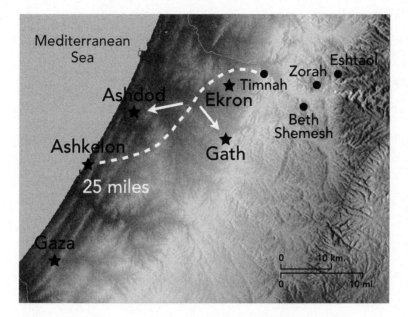

The wedding takes place at Timnah. In order for Samson to end up at Ashkelon, he would have exited the Sorek Valley on its western end, hung a left, and headed southwest toward Ekron, one of the cities of the Philistine Pentapolis (all five cities are present and demarcated with a star). What's perplexing is why Samson chooses to bypass Ekron and head all the way to Ashkelon in order to do his killing. Even if he didn't want to stop at Ekron, he could've chosen Ashdod or Gath. And yet he goes all the way to Ashkelon, twenty-five miles away from the wedding, in order to do his deed. Perhaps he didn't want to stir up a hornet's nest too close to home. But knowing the interconnected communications between the Philistine cities, word would have traveled quickly. Whether intentionally or incidentally, Samson simply made the hornet's nest much larger.

Burning with anger, he retraces his steps and heads home to Mahaneh Dan, likely bypassing Timnah and the cleanup crew along the way. Meanwhile, because it was believed the marriage was over, "Samson's wife was given to one of his companions who had attended him at the feast" (Judg. 14:20).

Goats, Jackals, and Donkey Jawbones

In Samson's mind the marriage isn't over. After some time, he heads back down the Sorek Valley to visit his wife and present her with a goat. (Who needs chocolate and roses when you can have a goat?) Samson arrives only to be told by his father-in-law that his wife is in the arms of one of his groomsmen—probably the best man. If that wasn't enough, Samson's father-in-law tries to pawn off a younger daughter as an acceptable replacement.

Refusing his father-in-law's offer, Samson does what any one of us would have done if we were in his sandals. He goes out and catches three hundred jackals,[11] ties their tails together in pairs, places torches in the knotted intersections of the tails, and sets the jackals loose in the fields around Timnah. Seriously, who comes up with that? Samson is an innovator. Let's at least give him that.

Although we'll circle back to this segment in greater detail in the next chapter, suffice it to say the results of Samson's escapades are devastating. The people are enraged. And once the damages are assessed and the culprit has been identified, the Philistine leaders of Timnah seek to eradicate the curse of Samson and his connection to Timnah by burning his wife and father-in-law to death. These Philistines aren't very nice people.

Samson responds to this unexpected retaliation by offering one of his own. According to the narrative, "He attacked them viciously and slaughtered many of them. Then he went down and stayed in a cave in the rock of Etam" (Judg. 15:8). Once again, Samson disregards the restrictions of his Nazirite vow, and kills an unidentified number of people. And then he ends up in a cave in the rock of Etam, eighteen miles to the southeast of Timnah, and less than two miles to the southwest of Bethlehem.

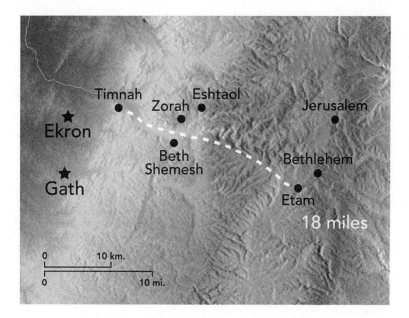

Alarmed at the sudden presence of more than a thousand Philistines in their region, three thousand men from Judah locate Samson and inquire of the circumstances. After becoming privy to the recent events, and concerned over Philistine retaliation, the men of Judah bind Samson with ropes and hand him over to their Philistine overlords near Lehi, an unidentified location in the vicinity of Etam.

But Samson doesn't go quietly. "As he approached Lehi, the Philistines came toward him shouting. The Spirit of the LORD came powerfully upon him. The ropes on his arms became like charred flax, and the bindings dropped from his hands. Finding a fresh jawbone of a donkey, he grabbed it and struck down a thousand men" (Judg. 15:14–15).

Samson has elevated his weaponry. He's gone from using his bare hands to a jawbone[12] of a donkey—and a "fresh" one no less. Now, even though it seems comical for the author to include this seemingly useless detail of "freshness," it's important. Remember, Nazirites aren't supposed to kill or be around dead things. A "fresh" jawbone carries the added detail of the donkey being recently deceased. For Samson to upgrade his weaponry, he would've likely had to remove the jawbone from the donkey's carcass, or at least been in the vicinity of the donkey's remains.

So not only does he kill a thousand men, but he also breaks the vow obtaining the weapon to kill the men. It's one offense on top of another. And in case you didn't pick up on it, the Spirit of the Lord shows up again at the front end of this killing spree. We'll address this later in the chapter, but until then we'll continue to sit in this tension.

Following this marvelous feat, at least in his eyes, Samson, the aspiring poet, breaks out with these words:

"With a donkey's jawbone
    I have made donkeys of them.
With a donkey's jawbone
    I have killed a thousand men." (Judges 15:16)

After taking all credit for himself, and then naming the place "Ramath Lehi" (which means "Jawbone Hill") after his accomplishment (see Judg. 15:17), Samson finds himself exhausted and thirsty. He cries out to the Lord for help by saying, "You have given your servant this great victory. Must I now die of thirst and fall into the hands of the uncircumcised?" (Judg. 15:18). This is the first time Samson acknowledges the LORD in the narrative, and it comes in a time of great need. God responds by miraculously providing water for Samson.

Life in Retirement

The next thing we know, it's twenty years later. As the end of Judges 15 puts it, "Samson led Israel for twenty years in the days of the Philistines" (v. 20). Samson apparently retires,[13] and in his retirement he seems to be running into boredom. So he heads to Gaza for a night on the town, and winds up hiring a prostitute for the night. This creates quite a stir in Gaza, for we read, "The people of Gaza were told, 'Samson is here!' So they surrounded the place and lay in wait for him all night at the city gate. They made no move during the night, saying, 'At dawn we'll kill him'" (Judg. 16:2). Why all the commotion? Once again, a map is helpful.

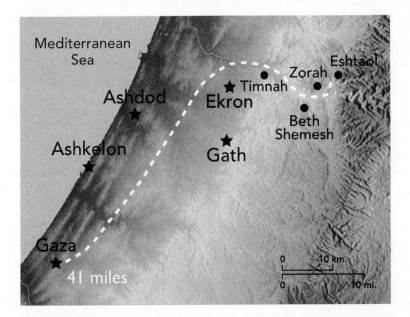

Assuming Samson began his journey from home, and took the most convenient and leisurely route to Gaza, he would've traveled forty-one miles, passing several Philistine cities along the way, including Timnah, where he burned up all the surrounding crops, and Ashkelon, where he struck down the thirty men. Gaza isn't just any city in the Philistine Pentapolis; it's the most important city of the Philistines. He goes right into the heart of Israel's arch nemesis. What's more, everyone knows who he is. He's been leading Israel for the last twenty years, and as the narrator highlights, "in the days of the Philistines," which is another way of saying, "in the days when the Philistines were strong." And yet Samson has kept the Philistines in check. He's been the bane of their existence. For twenty years, they've wanted Samson's head on a platter. So the moment it becomes public knowledge that Samson is in their city, the Philistines hatch a plan to rid themselves of this Israelite curse.

Knowing that his presence hasn't gone unnoticed, Samson rises in the middle of the night, and foils the Philistine plan. He then does the unimaginable. As the writer tells it, he "took hold of the doors of the city gate, together with the two posts, and tore them loose, bar and all. He lifted them to his shoulders and carried them to the top of the hill that faces Hebron" (Judg. 16:3).

City gates were enormous. They generally consisted of two large wooden doors that covered an area wide enough for chariots to pass through. Since they served as the only means of passing in and out of a walled city, they had to be constructed to withstand enemy assault. It has been estimated these gate doors weighed at least four to five hundred pounds,[14] and that may be a low estimate. Astonishingly, Samson rips out the doors, their adjoining posts, and the bar that locked the doors shut, and hauls them to the top of the hill facing Hebron. Hebron is forty miles away from Gaza, and over thirty-three hundred feet in elevation gain![15]

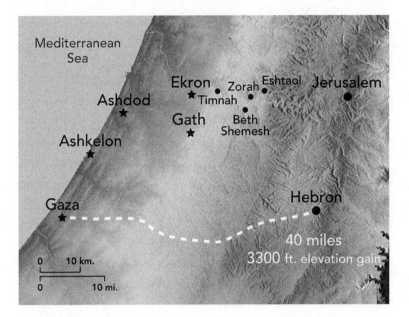

This isn't just an incredible feat. Samson is making a point. A city gate was the symbol of the city's protection. To conquer the city gate was to conquer the city. For Samson to destroy their city gate and haul it off as a trophy was his way of saying, "I still own you. Even the gate of your most important city doesn't stand a chance against me. And to prove it, I'm going to take your gate to the highest point in southern Israel as a testament to my strength and power over you!" Needless to say, the Philistines didn't take kindly to this humiliation.

And then comes the infamous story of Samson and Delilah, a story we'll look at in detail in Chapter 4. However, I'll draw out a few elements as we skim through this well-known section. Delilah is from the Sorek Valley, the same valley in which much of the Samson story unfolds. She is tasked by her Philistine counterparts to uncover the source of Samson's great strength. After three rounds of Samson toying with her, which includes bowstrings, ropes, and having his hair pinned into a loom, he gives in and reveals the source of his strength. As Samson tells it, "No razor has ever been used on my head because I have been a Nazirite dedicated to God from my mother's womb. If my head were shaved, my strength would leave me, and I would become as weak as any other man" (Judg. 16:17).

Unbeknownst to Samson, Delilah sends word to the Philistine rulers. While he is asleep on her lap, the rulers come in and silently remove the locks of Samson's hair, eliminating the source of his great strength. Perhaps you'll recall that a Nazirite isn't allowed to cut their hair. Although Samson has broken his vow several times, this is the first time in connection to this restriction. What we realize in this moment is that he's now broken his Nazirite vow from every possible angle.

After they shaved him and deprived him of his strength, "the Philistines seized him, gouged out his eyes and took him down to Gaza. Binding him with bronze shackles, they set him to grinding grain in the prison" (Judg. 16:21). Why Gaza? Again, it's the most important city. It's the heart of Philistine life, and now Samson has become their prized possession. The man who has been the bane of their existence and has humiliated them on numerous occasions has himself been humiliated by losing his eyes and being relegated to a blind prisoner who grinds grain.

For Samson there seems to be little hope at this point. However, what the narrator includes in the very next statement is telling. He writes, "But the hair on his head began to grow again after it had been shaved" (Judg. 16:22). A small detail the Philistines are going to regret overlooking.

Crashing the Party

In celebration of their victory over the mighty Samson, the Philistines hold a great celebration at the temple of Dagon, their patron deity. Three thousand Philistine men and women are present for the party, including all of the Philistine rulers. In the midst of the festivities, the people begin shouting for Samson to be paraded into the room and made to perform in some way. Some have suggested this may have included tripping him or beating him or placing obstacles in Samson's way and watching him grope about in disarray because of his blindness.[16]

After he has been put through this gauntlet of humiliation, there's a break in the action. Standing among the pillars of the temple, Samson gets an idea. Masking his intentions, he requests of the servant responsible for him, "Put me where I can feel the pillars that support the temple, so that I may lean against them" (Judg. 16:26). Thinking nothing of it, the servant obliges.

Stationed between the central supporting pillars of the temple complex, Samson prays, "Sovereign LORD, remember me. Please, God, strengthen me just once more, and let me with one blow get revenge on the Philistines for my two eyes" (Judg. 16:28). It's an interesting prayer because this is only the second time Samson acknowledges God in the narrative. And like the first, it comes in a time when he's in great need, making it seem as though God is of no value until he needs help. It's also interesting because it seems to be a prayer requesting God's blessing on his personal revenge.

Arriving at the culminating moment of the narrative, we read, "Then Samson reached toward the two central pillars on which the temple stood. Bracing himself against them, his right hand on the one and his left hand on the other, Samson said, 'Let me die with the Philistines!' Then he pushed with all his might, and down came the temple on the rulers and all the people in it. Thus he killed many more when he died than while he lived" (Judg. 16:29–30).[17]

The story concludes with, "Then his brothers and his father's whole family went down to get him. They brought him back and buried him between Zorah and Eshtaol in the tomb of Manoah his father. He had led Israel twenty years" (Judg. 16:31).

Samson goes to his grave breaking his Nazirite vow one last time. As you know full well, he's not allowed to kill. And yet three thousand men and women are ushered into death at the hands of Samson.

Which leads us to ask, "Then why did God answer Samson's prayer for strength to knock those pillars off their bases and break his Nazirite vow again by killing?"

We assume God answers Samson's prayer because of what happens. But the text never tells us that. What the text does tell us is that Samson's strength is connected to his hair, and while he's in prison, his hair begins growing back. Just because Samson prays a prayer doesn't mean God answers it, even if the end result is Samson's desire. God gave Samson a gift. His gift was his strength, connected to his hair. As long as he has his hair, he has his gift. And he can use that gift however he desires. That's the nature of the gifts we possess. We can use them for good or we can use them for ill.

Furthermore, notice there was no mention of the Spirit of the LORD coming upon Samson is this final scene. In fact, there hasn't been a single mention of it for the last chapter in Judges. The last time we hear about the Spirit coming upon Samson is when Samson kills the thousand men near Lehi with the jawbone.

This has created a lot of confusion in the Samson story. Now that we have an overarching understanding of the larger narrative, I'll spend the rest of this chapter addressing this issue in an attempt to bring clarity, because I believe what's being communicated with the Spirit of the LORD is absolutely foundational to how we understand the Samson story.

The Spirit of the LORD

Many have believed or understood it's the Spirit of the LORD who infuses Samson with strength in order to accomplish the incredible feats he does. But here's where the argument begins to crumble. There are ten feats that Samson performs in the book of Judges. In only three of these feats is there any mention of the Spirit. There is no mention of the Spirit in the other seven.

Mention of the Spirit of the LORD	No Mention of the Spirit of the LORD
Killing the Lion (14:6)	Capturing Jackals and Burning Crops (15:4–5)
Killing the 30 Men of Ashkelon (14:19)	Killing the Men of Timnah (15:8)
Killing the 1,000 Men near Lehi (15:14–15)	Tearing Off Gate and Trekking to Hebron (16:3)
	Escaping from the Bowstrings (16:9)
	Escaping from the Ropes (16:12)
	Escaping from the Loom (16:14)
	Killing the 3,000 Men and Women in the Temple (16:30)

As we know from the story, Samson says to Delilah, "No razor has ever been used on my head because I have been a Nazirite dedicated to God from my mother's womb. If my head were shaved, my strength would leave me, and I would become as weak as any other man" (Judg. 16:17). By Samson's own admission, his strength is connected to his hair. He never says anything about his strength being connected to the Spirit of the LORD. So what's problematic isn't the lack of the Spirit's presence in seven of these feats, but its showing up in three of them, and seemingly empowering Samson to break his vow, which is in direct opposition to God's desire.

But the Spirit of the LORD cannot be in opposition to God. Therefore, to make sense of what's going on, we must look at the Hebrew behind the English. I understand this may feel a bit technical, and you may have never encountered the Hebrew language before, but the answer is in the language.

Ancient Hebrew is very different from English. As my friend Lois Tverberg describes it, "Hebrew is a 'word-poor' language. Biblical Hebrew includes only about 8,000 words, far fewer than the 400,000 or more we have in English. Paradoxically, the richness of Hebrew comes from its poverty. Because the ancient language has so few words, each one is like an overstuffed suitcase, bulging with extra meanings that it must carry in order for the language to fully describe reality."[18] This is why we have so many English translations. There are many options translating from Hebrew to English. Owing to this reality, we must keep in mind that every translation is an interpretation. What one believes is going on in a passage will determine how one translates the passage, since multiple options are generally on the table.

Translators are brilliant. Without their ability to translate from the original languages, most of the world wouldn't be able to read the Bible, myself included. So gratitude and humility must run hand in hand with any critique. With that in mind, I'd like to suggest that most translations haven't adequately captured the Hebrew and the context of the passages when it comes to the Spirit of the LORD's involvement in the Samson story.

Remember, there are three instances when the Spirit shows up and Samson kills. The language construction in each of these instances is all the same in Hebrew. So in dealing with one, we'll understand all three. Most intriguing is the first one. Remember the lion scene? Let's read it again.

As they approached the vineyards of Timnah, suddenly a young lion came roaring toward him. The Spirit of the LORD came powerfully upon him so that he tore the lion apart with his bare hands as he might have torn a young goat. But he told neither his father nor his mother what he had done. (Judges 14:5–6)

The Hebrew verb translated as "powerfully" is *tzalach*, which can mean "to rush, prosper, succeed, or be powerful."[19] With Hebrew definitions, the context of a passage dictates which meaning is intended or is most likely. However, nuances of each meaning can be present in the context, which is what I believe is going on here in the lion story, since the meanings can be closely related. *Tzalach* is the idea of something coming quickly (i.e., rushing) upon someone or something, and doing so powerfully, which means it's prospering and therefore succeeding in the process. In this case, it's the Spirit of the Lord coming upon Samson. Because of the immediacy of the lion's presence and the response Samson must generate, I believe it's most accurate and helpful to translate *tzalach* from the "rushing" aspect of the definition, which is exactly how the New Revised Standard Version renders it. Therefore, translating the line as "The Spirit of the Lord rushed upon him . . ."

Now, the Spirit of the Lord comes on a lot of people in the Bible. But the specific Hebrew phrase used in connection with *tzalach* in this passage—*alav ruach YHWH*[20] (literally, "upon him the Spirit of the Lord")—only shows up eight times[21] in the Bible (three of which are in our Samson story).[22] Of the eight times, one passage actually defines what the Spirit is doing. In Isaiah 11:2, we read, "The Spirit of the Lord will rest on him—the Spirit of wisdom and of understanding, the Spirit of counsel and of might, the Spirit of the knowledge and fear of the Lord." There's only one Spirit of the Lord. So the reference here in Isaiah 11:2 is to the same Spirit as in the Samson story.

One more piece, and then we'll put these Hebrew language connections together.

In the Judges passage above, we're told the Spirit of the Lord rushes upon him [Samson] "so that he tore the lion apart..." The "so that" makes it appear it's the Spirit's rushing upon Samson that causes him to kill the lion. Meaning, God's Spirit is the one responsible for Samson violating his Nazirite vow. The problem is, "so that" is not in the original Hebrew. The translators added it in not because the translation warranted it, but because of their interpretation of what they believed the Spirit was doing.[23] The Hebrew does not have "so that" but "and." The translation should read, "The Spirit of the LORD rushed upon him, *and* he tore the lion apart..."[24] The Hebrew is not saying the Spirit is responsible for causing Samson to tear the lion apart and thus violate his Nazirite vow. It's saying Samson tears the lion apart of his own accord.

In light of the Hebrew language and the overall narrative of the Samson story, what's going on here now begins to make sense. In three different instances, when Samson's about to break his Nazirite vow by killing, the Spirit of the LORD—a Spirit of wisdom, understanding, counsel, might, knowledge, and fear of the LORD—rushes upon Samson and confronts him by essentially saying, "Samson, think about what you're about to do. You've been called to be a Nazirite, to set a Godly example for your peers and for the world at large. Be faithful. Don't do what you're about to do."

Samson's response?

"And he tore the lion apart."
"And he went down to Ashkelon and struck down thirty of their men."
"And finding a fresh jawbone of a donkey, he grabbed it and struck down a thousand men."

In each of the three instances when the Spirit of the LORD races upon the scene to confront him, Samson blatantly disregards the

Spirit's plea. The LORD is confronting Samson because He cares for him and wants to challenge his thinking. He desires Samson to reconsider his actions. But Samson wants none of it. He does what he wants to do. And in each case he kills someone or something, violating his God-ordained Nazirite vow.

When Lions Approach

It's one thing to unpack the Hebrew language and understand that Samson kills the lion of his own accord. It's another thing to take his circumstances into consideration. There's a lion on the scene, for crying out loud. It makes you wonder what Samson was supposed to do.

A helpful place to begin is to look at other lion stories in the Bible. Oftentimes, stories with similar elements can shed light on the story you're dealing with. It turns out there are a few stories about lions that do.

In 1 Kings 13, we read about a prophet of God who disregards God's instructions, and God sends a lion that mauls the man (and yet leaves his donkey alone, just to show the incident wasn't a fluke). A few chapters later, in 1 Kings 20, there is another story about a prophet of God who apparently disobeys God's word and a lion is sent to kill him.[25] And although he's using it metaphorically, the prophet Jeremiah highlights the lion as a means of judgment upon the leaders of Judah in Jeremiah 5.[26]

So we have at least three instances where the lion serves as a symbol of confrontation and judgment. Perhaps that's what's going on in our story. Notice again how the scene begins. "As they approached the vineyards of Timnah, suddenly a young lion came roaring toward him." The details here are revealing.

The lion comes out of Timnah's vineyards. According to his Nazirite restrictions, Samson is supposed to stay away from vineyards.

What's more, the reason he's even in the vicinity of one is because he's on his way to directly disobey God by marrying a Philistine woman.

The presence of the lion makes sense. It's there to confront Samson on the path he's going—to give him a chance to turn around and walk the other way (both literally and figuratively). His life is heading in the wrong direction. He is not living into his identity and calling. And God uses a lion as a means to confront him.

But not just any lion. Once again, the details are paramount. The latter half of Judges 14:5 literally reads from the Hebrew, "and look, a young lion of lions came roaring toward him." This is the only place in the entire Old Testament where the phrase "young lion of lions" is used. The writer has gone out of his way to emphasize this is a "young lion." Perhaps it's a cub. We don't know. The point is Samson's life doesn't appear to be in immediate danger. The young lion isn't attacking him, but roaring at him. He can choose to walk away. He can choose a different path. This scene is not about Samson's strength. It's about God's leading, and Samson's refusal to follow.

If his life had been in danger and his act had been in self-defense, then why not tell his parents? I don't know about you, but if I had just killed a lion in self-defense, I would've said to my parents, "Hey, I just killed a lion." But he doesn't because he knows he's not supposed to kill the young lion. His act was not in self-defense. It was in defiance of the Spirit's counsel to walk away.

This is foundational to the Samson narrative. On three different occasions, the Spirit of the LORD rushes upon the scene and confronts Samson about the choices before him. And on all three occasions, Samson essentially says to the Spirit, "Get lost," and then he proceeds to do what he wants.

How often do we find ourselves about to make an errant decision, and an inner voice of reason rushes upon us and confronts us on what we're about to do?

"Don't go into that bar. It won't be only one drink."

"Don't say it. It will only make matters worse."

"Stay away from that website. You know where it'll lead."

"Keep all your fingers on the steering wheel. They cut you off. Let it go."

"You're not telling the whole truth. Come clean."

"Don't turn on the television. It's late and you know you won't end up watching just SportsCenter or QVC."

"Don't hit 'Send' on that e-mail. You'll regret it."

"Think about how this will affect your family. It's not worth it."

"Don't buy it. You don't need it, and you don't have the money to cover it."

I would argue that that inner voice of reason is the Spirit of God speaking into our lives, seeking to help us by pleading with us to avoid decisions that will inject unnecessary pain and discouragement into our lives. And in these moments, we have a choice. We can heed the Spirit's counsel or we can tell the Spirit to get lost. Everything within us will want to choose the latter. But we can choose the former. As the apostle Paul articulates in a letter to the residents of Corinth, "No temptation has overtaken you except what is common to mankind. And God is faithful; he will not let you be tempted beyond what you can bear. But when you are tempted, he will also provide a way out so that you can endure it" (1 Cor. 10:13). There's always a way out. Sometimes we're so entrenched in the moment, we don't think about our options. It's in these moments the Spirit of the Lord rushes upon us and confronts us with our options.

Here's what's scary about all of this. The more we tell the Spirit to get lost, the less we sense the Spirit rushing upon us. We become desensitized. Our hearts become hard and our ears become blocked. Consequently, we venture down paths that become increasingly destructive. Oftentimes, we don't even realize who we've become as a result of it.

I believe this is what happens to Samson in our story. Over and over again, he rejects the Spirit speaking into his life, and makes decisions based on what he wants. As we'll continue to explore, those decisions have devastating results. Everything begins going downhill the moment we become privy to Samson's apathetic attitude toward God's calling for his life and his rejection of the Spirit's plea to get back on track.

We've all experienced this in our lives. His struggle is our struggle. We have times when we get off track and lose our way. We have times when we tell the Spirit to get lost when confronted on the road we're plowing. We know what it's like to live out of tune with what's healthy and good for our lives. This is precisely why I believe the Samson story was told. It wasn't told just because it's true, or because it had significant ramifications for the Israelites at a precarious time in their history. I believe it was told in order to instruct us on how to live in tune with God by being confronted with all the many ways Samson failed to do so. His story is meant to teach us. His mistakes are to be our lessons. Samson was called to be a Nazirite—a quintessential example of someone in sync with the desires of God. He was called to embody the human experience of how one relates well with the God of the universe. And yet he didn't live into his calling. He missed his purpose. He got things wrong.

We each have a calling upon our lives. For some it's to be a teacher. For others it's to be a salesman, a stay-at-home parent, a nurse, a financial analyst, a janitor, a professional athlete, a painter, a bus driver, a politician, or whatever. These callings vary from person to person. Although we'll spend a chapter discussing individual callings like those above, this book is intended to explore the more universal callings of humanity to maximize the human experience by living healthy, dynamic, and meaningful lives. Although Samson had an individual calling to address the oppression of the Philistines (see Judg. 13:5) his Nazirite calling was to embody the universal characteristics of someone living out God's desires and teachings. Therefore, the more we understand the life of Samson, and where he got things wrong, the more we'll understand where we need to get things right to flourish in our humanity, to make the most of the lives we've been given, and to leave a positive mark on our world.

As tragic as the Samson story is, it's a gift. Seeing the causes and effects of poorly made decisions from another's life helps us make changes in our own. There is much to be gleaned from this ancient story. The wisdom and instructions contained have vast implications for our lives. It's my desire that as we continue to unpack this remarkable story, the Spirit of the LORD will rush upon us all, and accompany us along this journey, confronting us on the many ways we haven't been living into the healthiness of our humanity, and giving us the hope, courage, and strength to fully live into the purposes for which we've been created.

CHAPTER 3

Seventy-Seven Times

Driving in Israel is similar to driving in the States. You drive on the right side of the road. You have clearly defined lines that indicate when you can pass and when you can't. The stop signs are red and octagonal in shape. And the stoplights flash green, yellow, and red.

However, there are some unique features. Whereas the centerlines dividing traffic in the States are yellow and the side margin lines are white, in Israel these colors are reversed. The stop signs do not feature the word "STOP," but simply display a hand facing the driver. And the transition to a red light entails the green light blinking three times (one blink per second), and then turning solid yellow for three seconds, followed by the light finally turning red. Essentially, you are given six seconds to prepare for a red light, which makes it difficult to rationalize to a police officer, "I didn't realize it would turn red so quickly."

Perhaps the most unique feature of Israeli driving is flocks. Countless times my wife and I encountered sheep and goats in the middle of the road. It became comical. At times we'd see the flock in the distance and have the luxury of slowly applying our brakes. Other times we'd crest a hill or come around a sharp bend and have to slam on the brakes. You always had to be on the lookout, because hitting a goat or a sheep is not like hitting a deer. The obvious differences of size and weight aside, deer are the property of nature. Sheep and goats are the property of people. And after hearing a true story about an accident involving a flock, I was even more cautious driving in Israel.

Several years ago, a driver with a busload of tourists was cruising along a road. It was a spectacular day, and the passengers were anticipating their next experience. Little did they know it would happen sooner than expected.

Climbing a steep hill that did not lend visibility past its crest, the bus driver had no way of knowing a flock was crossing the road ahead. After cresting the hill, and seeing the flock, he immediately jumped on the brakes. However, it was too late. The mass of the bus couldn't overcome the laws of physics and plowed into the flock. After the bloodstained bus came to a stop and the survey of damage was completed, over thirty sheep and goats were dead or injured. Yes, it was a bloodbath. Fortunately, the shepherd had already crossed the road and the carnage didn't claim any human lives.

Shaken by the incident, and grappling with the ramifications, the bus driver exited the bus, profusely apologizing to the shepherd. Granted, the bus driver was not at fault. Anyone driving that bus would have suffered the same fate. So why the profuse apology? Because this is the Middle East.

After several failed apologies, the bus driver said, "I'll reimburse you for everything you've lost," an outlandish offer from one who wasn't at fault and an offer that would require significant funds. To which the shepherd replied, "I don't want your money in exchange for the blood of my sheep and goats. I want your blood instead!"

Not every accident like this in the Middle East proceeds in this way. But an incident like this reflects a certain mentality. It's a mentality that believes if you're wronged or hurt by someone, the only appropriate response is to exact a punishment beyond what was done to you, and somehow that makes things even. In the shepherd's mind, the only way to resolve the situation wasn't with financial compensation to recoup his loss, but with the death of the bus driver. It's a barbaric way of thinking, and yet it's been around for a long, long time.

When Brides Are Given to Best Men

As we explored in Chapter 2, Samson's first encounter with death is a young lion on his way to Timnah. Disregarding the Spirit's counsel, Samson shreds the lion to pieces and makes a riddle out of it during his wedding feast.

The riddle gets solved (thanks to his wife), and Samson loses the bet. Disregarding the Spirit's counsel yet again, he storms off to Ashkelon and kills thirty men. Stripping them of their clothes, he heads back to Timnah and settles his debt. Boiling with anger, Samson returns back to Mahaneh Dan alone.

This brings us to Judges 15, where the effects of these two prior events begin to mount. The chapter opens, "Later on, at the time of wheat harvest, Samson took a young goat and went to visit his wife. He said, 'I'm going to my wife's room.' But her father would not let him go in" (v. 1).

As we saw in Chapter 2, Samson's father-in-law assumes the marriage is over, and subsequently gives his daughter to one of Samson's companions (again, probably the best man). Which makes sense. Well, maybe not the part of him giving his daughter to another dude, but the part of assuming the marriage is over. Samson did kill thirty men as a result of losing a bet due to his daughter's actions, and then left her alone in Timnah while returning home. Furthermore, the father says he thought Samson "hated" his daughter (see Judg. 15:2). "Hate" is the Hebrew word *sānē*, which carried divorce implications in the Ancient Near East.[1]

Samson becomes irate. Disregarding his father-in-law's suggestion to take his younger daughter instead, Samson makes an explosive statement. He says, "This time I have a right to get even with the Philistines; I will really harm them" (Judg. 15:3).

Someone does him wrong, and he immediately feels justified in retaliating. That's revenge.

"Revenge is the action of inflicting hurt or harm on someone for an injury or wrong suffered at their hands."[2] Samson believes he's been wronged. He's angry with his father-in-law, and he wants justice. According to his statement, he's going to administer the vengeance because he has "a right to get even." Interesting choice of words he uses.

Samson wants justice because his wife was given to another guy as a result of his storming off and murdering thirty Philistine men for losing a silly bet—a bet, may I remind you, made possible only by the fact that Samson blatantly broke his Nazirite vow.

This is what's scary about exacting revenge. We get so bent on "getting even," we fail to take into consideration the larger story and our part in it. We begin to believe our retaliation is justifiable and innocent. In fact, the Hebrew word translated as "get even" in Samson's statement above is *naqah*, which means, "to be innocent or blameless."[3] In Samson's mind, irrespective of his preceding actions, he not only has a right to administer vengeance, but he'll remain blameless in his retaliation. This is a frightening train of thought.

"Getting even" for Samson looks like going out and catching three hundred jackals and tying their tails together. After the tail-tying act, we're told, "He then fastened a torch to every pair of tails, lit the torches and let the foxes loose in the standing grain of the

Philistines. He burned up the shocks and standing grain, together with the vineyards and olive groves" (Judg. 15:4–5).

Crops in Israel fall into two main categories: winter crops and summer crops. To mention "shocks and standing grain" is to reference the winter crops, which consisted of wheat and barley. Harvested in late spring and early summer, these were known as the winter crops because they matured during the winter months (rainy season). To mention "vineyards and olive groves" was to reference the summer crops, which matured during the summer months (dry season) and were harvested late summer and early fall. They consisted of other crops, such as figs, almonds, dates, and pomegranates, but grapes and olives were the most important—hence, their mention here.

To be told Samson's antics "burned up the shocks and the standing grain, together with the vineyards and olives groves" is to be informed Samson destroyed both their winter and their summer crops, which in an agricultural-based society means Samson has decimated their economy, livelihood, and food supply. Not only is this wrong from a humanitarian perspective, but it's wrong from a biblical perspective. According to God's commandment found in Exodus 22:6, "If a fire breaks out and spreads into thornbushes so that it burns shocks of grain or standing grain or the whole field, the one who started the fire must make restitution." Clearly Samson has no intention to make restitution. He's thrilled with the mayhem.

Unable to harm the man responsible, and seeking revenge for this catastrophe, the Philistines resort to burning Samson's wife and father-in-law to death. You begin to see the kind of people these Philistines are. They're hard-nosed, no-nonsense, tough-minded people, who will relentlessly defend their honor, no matter how repugnant the tactic.

What began as a simple dispute between Samson and his

father-in-law has quickly escalated into an entire city losing their source of livelihood, and two people being burned alive. Apparently, this is what "getting even" looks like for Samson, whose actions are blameless in his eyes.

But he's not finished. In fact, he's just getting warmed up.

In response to this Philistine retaliation, Samson states, "Since you act like this, I will surely take revenge on you, but after that I will quit" (Judg. 15:7, NASB). Seriously? "Since *you* act like this"... because setting the valley on fire was a mature and civilized response to a personal dispute.

Notice how Samson's shifting the blame. He's demonizing the actions of the others (which, let's be honest, were gruesome) while maintaining his own innocence. And since he's been wronged and believes he has a right to get even, this justifies another round of revenge. Additionally, he believes that this next round will quench his vengeance thirst because, he contends, "after that I will quit."

It's not that easy. Samson has an inflated sense of his own control. This is what revenge does to us. It makes us believe we can engage it and quit whenever we want. The problem is, we can't. Revenge is alluring and intoxicating. It gets into our blood and takes over. We don't control it. It controls us. This is why Samson's statement, "after that I will quit," is laughable. It's unrealistic. It's a myth. It's a form of justification, because the reality doesn't hold true. Revenge begets revenge.

The gas in the engine of revenge is the belief that if you hit the opposition back hard enough, they won't retaliate. This is exactly what Samson is attempting to do here. The Philistines hit him. Now he's going to hit back harder, believing they'll just roll over and call it quits. The problem is, the Philistines are operating under the same assumption. Once they get hit, they'll strike back harder so Samson will call it quits. It's the classic escalating cycle of revenge.

This is precisely the mentality and reality God seeks to address when He provides instructions in the Torah[4] for what's often referred to as *lex talionis* (a Latin phrase meaning "the law of retaliation"), which was intended to serve the purpose of retributive justice, but had strict limitations. *Lex talionis* stipulated if someone incurs an injury at the hands of another, the victim is allowed to exact revenge only for the extent to which they suffered, and nothing more. This was their legal expression of our modern law, which states the punishment should fit the crime. This is first seen in Exodus 21:24 with instructions for an "eye for eye, tooth for tooth, hand for hand, foot for foot."[5]

Lex talionis's purpose was to eliminate the escalation of violence pervasive in the social fabric of society. Without such a law, revenge would always escalate. If you break my arm, I'll kill your daughter. That's how it was. Therefore, *lex talionis* was a form of grace. It limited what could be exacted, therefore reducing the chaos and pain that would ensue from retribution for an injury or tragedy.[6] It was a one-time, one-act, legal response to something that was done to you, and overseen by judicial officials, all for the purpose of crippling the revenge cycle.[7] Samson has no reverence for such a purpose. Therefore, what ensues in the story shouldn't surprise us a bit.

In response to the Philistine retaliation, Samson "attacked them viciously and slaughtered many of them. Then he went down and stayed in a cave in the rock of Etam" (Judg. 15:8). Samson once again breaks his Nazirite vow by ruthlessly killing an unidentified number of Philistines, and then flees eighteen miles in the opposite direction to Lehi. The Philistines follow Samson to the region of Judah and lie in wait.

As you might imagine, the people of Judah are alarmed by the sudden influx of Philistines in their region, and thus inquire of their purpose. "We have come to take Samson prisoner and to do to him as he did to us" (Judg. 15:10). Now privy to the circumstances, we are told three thousand men from Judah go looking for Samson in the cave in the rock of Etam.

Samson's actions have pulled an additional *three thousand* people into the mix. Revenge also has a way of doing this. The longer it goes on, the more people get sucked into the vortex. For Samson, this vortex is growing substantially—both geographically as well as numerically. Now spanning the real estate from Ashkelon to Etam, it includes both enemies and countrymen.

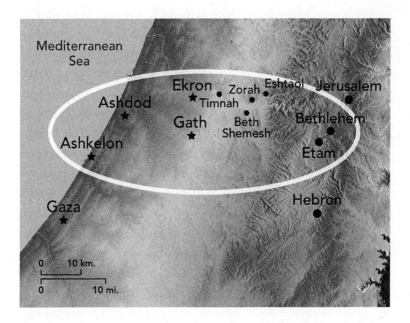

What began as a civil dispute has escalated into an issue of national security—for both the Philistines and the Israelites. At this particular moment in history, the Philistines are ruling the Israelites. Upsetting your oppressors comes with grave consequences, and the men of Judah want nothing of it. Finding Samson, they express their concern by exclaiming, "Don't you realize that the Philistines are rulers over us? What have you done to us?" (Judg. 15:11).

Samson's response is classic. In fact, it could've been the epitaph on his gravestone (if they had them in Samson's time). For he claims, "I merely did to them what they did to me" (Judg. 15:11). Notably, the writer lets his words sit in midair. There's no commentary. No explanation. No rebuttal from the men of Judah. Samson's justification indicates he's so entangled in revenge he's completely lost touch with reality. It's not even worth discussing.

Dismissing his pathetic claim as rubbish, the men of Judah disclose their plan to hand him over to the Philistines. They want the violence to end, and this appears to be their only option. With Samson's consent, they bind him with two new ropes and head in the direction of the Philistines.

But as quickly as the plan is concocted, it's abandoned. For as we read, "As he approached Lehi, the Philistines came toward him shouting. The Spirit of the LORD rushed upon him.[8] And the ropes on his arms became like charred flax, and the bindings dropped from his hands. Finding a fresh jawbone of a donkey, he grabbed it and struck down a thousand men" (Judg. 15:14). And once again, Samson breaks his Nazirite vow in order to continue his pursuit of revenge. This isn't the last time we'll see the cycle of revenge in the story.

Fast-forward twenty years. Samson's at it again with his presence in Gaza. As we explored in Chapter 2, he embarrasses the Philistines yet again by taking their city gate and rendering their mighty city conquered. Seeking revenge for this incident, and for twenty years of humiliation, they employ the seductive Delilah to discover the source of Samson's strength. After several rounds of toying with her, Samson finally gives in and discloses the source of his strength. Acting upon the intelligence, the Philistines cut his hair, gouge out his eyes, and haul him off to Gaza.

After an undisclosed period of time, the Philistines hold a victory celebration in the temple of their patron deity—Dagon. As the image of Dagon is paraded out, the people break out in boisterous cheers and praise their god by saying, "Our god has delivered our enemy into our hands, the one who laid waste our land and multiplied our slain" (Judg. 16:24). The reference to their slain countrymen is to be expected. Samson has killed well over a thousand of them. But take notice also of the implicit reference to their crops being destroyed. The jackal incident was a big deal, not only because it impoverished their economy and stripped them of food, but because it demoralized Dagon, who was also known as the grain god. With Samson's capture, Dagon has avenged the Philistine losses of land and men, and has demonstrated his ability to prevail over the Philistine enemies.

But it's short lived. After being humiliated himself in front of three thousand men and women, Samson gets placed between two of the temple's supporting pillars. With hair on his head, and a plan in his mind, he prays, "Sovereign LORD, remember me. Please, God, strengthen me just once more, and let me with one blow get revenge on the Philistines for my two eyes" (Judg. 16:28).

What's interesting is how hopeful this prayer begins. When he says, "Sovereign LORD, remember me. Please, God, strengthen me once more," it appears he's coming around—as if he's finally recognizing his failings and sincerely wants to salvage some aspect of his dignity and calling to do what God desires.

Yet what comes next obliterates any such notion. For he crescendos with, "and let me with one blow get revenge on the Philistines for my two eyes." Sadly, nothing has changed. Samson still has vengeance in his veins, and is still only thinking of himself. He wants revenge for the humiliation he's suffered at the hands of the Philistines, and he's seeking to employ God for his personal vendetta. That's the point of his prayer. He could care less about doing anything for God or others. It's about him. Lest we think otherwise, notice why he wants revenge—"for my two eyes." Samson's been disgraced with the loss of his eyes, and he's seeking revenge to regain his honor.

When other figures of the Bible ask God for help to do something significant, they do so for God's honor and not their own. When David fights Goliath, he does so in order that "the whole world will know that there is a God in Israel" (1 Sam. 17:46). When Solomon is dedicating the temple and pleading with God to hear the prayers of the people, he says, "so that all the peoples of the earth may know your name and fear you" (1 Kings 8:43). When Elijah is dueling with the Baal prophets on Mount Carmel, he fervently cries out, "Answer me, LORD, answer me, so these people will know that you, LORD, are God, and that you are turning their hearts back again" (1 Kings 18:37). When Hezekiah asks for God's deliverance in the midst of the Assyrian siege, he says, "so that all the kingdoms of the earth may know that you alone, LORD, are God" (2 Kings 19:19). When Samson asks for God's assistance, he does so in order to get revenge on the loss of his eyes and regain his personal honor.

This is why I'm not convinced God answers his prayer. Samson's strength was connected to his hair, and we're told, "the hair on his head began to grow again after it had been shaved" (Judg. 16:22). When Samson's in the temple complex, he has enough strength to execute his plan. He's just not sure of it. So to ensure his revenge, he asks for God's help.[9] Which means, he is specifically asking God to bless his epic act of revenge and the breaking of his Nazirite vow one last time.

And then we come to the culminating moment of the narrative. "Then Samson reached toward the two central pillars on which the temple stood. Bracing himself against them, his right hand on the one and his left hand on the other, Samson said, 'Let me die with the Philistines!' Then he pushed with all his might, and down came the temple on the rulers and all the people in it. Thus he killed many more when he died than while he lived" (Judg. 16:29–30).

1—30—?—1,000—3,000

It begins with a single lion. It moves to thirty men of Ashkelon. It progresses to the slaughtering of an unidentified number of people (?).[10] It advances to a thousand men near Lehi. It then culminates with three thousand men and women at the temple of Dagon in Gaza, including himself. Every subsequent killing is more destructive than the previous. The writer is helping us see the escalation of violence inherent in the Samson narrative. From a single animal to three thousand men and women, Samson's revenge and violence escalates until it kills him.

This is the trajectory of revenge when the cycle continues unbroken. It's lethal, and it's barbaric. And the writer is doing everything in his power to demonstrate what happens when we give in to the alluring nature of revenge and how it can derail our lives.

For some of us, Samson's story is deeply convicting. Others of us read a story like Samson's and think, "Wow, I'm so glad I'm not like that." Or we hear a story about a shepherd who wants the blood of a man for accidentally killing his animals, and we're appalled by such rationale. And yet how often do we do the same thing? How often do we exact a punishment beyond what was done to us? How often do we get back at someone for something they did to us? Maybe our revenge doesn't look like Samson's, but we know how to get back at the people around us.

We give the silent treatment or turn the cold shoulder.

We post something cruel or incriminating on Facebook or another social media platform.

We pass along gossip regardless of whether it's true or not.

We make derogatory comments about a boss after a poor performance review.

We craft a deeply penetrating e-mail that rips the recipient to shreds.

We go for the jugular with words in a heated exchange.

We cut someone off in traffic.

We shut someone out of a will.

We get as elaborate as doctoring a lawsuit against someone for something they didn't do.

Or we go so far as to inflict physical harm with our fists or some other object of destruction.

Every time we seek to get back at someone for something done to us, we exhibit the same barbaric mentality of the shepherd and of Samson. It's kind of a sobering thought.

Letting God Do His Job

We all know what it's like to be wronged. It's painful and enraging. In those moments, our propensity is to exact revenge—to get back at someone for what they've done to us. It's a normal human inclination. But as we've seen, acting upon it is destructive. There's no redeeming value to personal revenge. And yet the last thing we want to do is to remain idle. We have a desire to respond. In fact, we intuitively understand we must respond. But our response must be appropriate and redemptive if anything good is going to come out of the situation. We need a framework for such a response.

In his letter to the followers of Jesus living in Rome, Paul addresses the issue of revenge when he writes, "Do not repay anyone evil for evil. Be careful to do what is right in the eyes of everyone. If it is possible, as far as it depends on you, live at peace with everyone. Do not take revenge, my dear friends, but leave room for God's wrath, for it is written: 'It is mine to avenge; I will repay,' says the Lord" (Rom. 12:17–19).

Notice Paul doesn't negate the need for revenge. He doesn't push it aside and say it isn't necessary. The reason is because revenge is actually a legal term.[11] It's a form of justice. It's the judgment or punishment levied against a perpetrator. Thus, the idea of revenge, in and of itself, isn't wrong. It's how it's administered and by whom that makes it positive or negative. This distinction is significant because oftentimes our driving force for seeking revenge is our need for justice. We have a sense of what is right and wrong (even though our scales may be skewed), and when our rights have been violated, we want justice. We don't want our perpetrator getting away scot-free. And when we don't believe there is anyone who will avenge the evil done to us, we take matters into our own hands.

But Paul reminds us that the evil done against us doesn't go unnoticed. God is profoundly aware of our situations, and will administer justice according to His perfect wisdom and unclouded judgment. It's why Paul says, "leave room for God's wrath," because God's wrath precedes the administering of His justice. God is a God of justice and promises to act, even though we may not appreciate His timing.

Furthermore, Paul reminds us vengeance isn't ours to execute. It's God's.[12] When we overstep our bounds, the resulting act is rarely, if ever, just. It's why Paul mentions not repaying "evil with evil," because he understands our response will take the form of evil, regardless of how justified we think it will be.[13]

Beyond that, the larger issue with revenge is when we step in and play the role of the avenger, it's as if we're telling God we're able to do His job better than He can.[14] It's telling Him we don't trust Him with our situation, and He can go find something else to do, because we'll handle it. To take revenge is to take the place of God. When we are wronged, the invitation is for us to trust that God is fully capable of doing His job, and to allow Him to do what only He's capable of doing correctly.

Even Jesus submitted to this reality. As Peter writes, "When they hurled their insults at him, he did not retaliate; when he suffered, he made no threats. Instead, he entrusted himself to him who judges justly" (1 Pet. 2:23). Jesus didn't take matters into His own hands. Even while He's being arrested, He says to Peter, who has just cut off the ear of the high priest's servant in retaliation, "Put your sword back in its place, for all who draw the sword will die by the sword. Do you think I cannot call on my Father, and he will at once put at my disposal more than twelve legions of angels?" (Matt. 26:52–53). With more than seventy-two thousand angels at His disposal, Jesus chooses not to retaliate. He chooses to entrust Himself to God. And we are to do the same.

Jesus makes this clear in His famous *Sermon on the Mount* teaching when He says, "You have heard that it was said, 'Eye for eye, and tooth for tooth.' But I tell you, do not resist an evil person" (Matt. 5:38–39). Addressing *lex talionis*, Jesus advocates His followers not to exact any form of vengeance. What's more, Jesus goes on to discuss three responses to someone who's seeking to harm you that pursue wholeness and restoration to the broken situations. So not only does Jesus not advocate for revenge, He offers redemptive ways of helping the opposing party.[15]

Jesus then begins the next portion of His teaching by saying, "You have heard that it was said, 'Love your neighbor and hate your enemy.' But I tell you, love your enemies and pray for those who persecute you" (Matt. 5:43–44). Part of Jesus' words here are a direct quote from the end of Leviticus 19:18, which states, "Love your neighbor as yourself." Interestingly, the entire verse reads, "Do not seek revenge or bear a grudge against anyone among your people, but love your neighbor as yourself. I am the LORD." Even though God allowed for *lex talionis* in the Old Testament, we see here in this passage that God's heart in the matter would be that His people would not respond with revenge. Jesus, who is expounding for the people the heart of God in His teaching, affirms this. Jesus is very interested in His followers not only refusing to retaliate or take revenge on someone, but to love them well in the midst of it all, just like His Father does.

We see the highest expression of Jesus demonstrating this at the end of His life. Picking up on the discussion above, not only does Jesus refuse to retaliate against the evil that was done against Him, but He responds in the most astounding of ways. While hanging on a bloodied cross, He says, "Father, forgive them, for they do not know what they are doing" (Luke 23:34). By entrusting Himself to God, and removing Himself from the role of the avenger, Jesus opens up the door for forgiveness, and boldly walks through. For Jesus, the redemptive and loving response to those who have wronged us is not revenge, but forgiveness.

Seventy-Seven Times

In Matthew's biography on the life of Jesus, a riveting exchange between Jesus and His disciples is recorded on this subject of forgiveness. Peter asks Jesus, "Lord, how many times shall I forgive my brother or sister who sins against me? Up to seven times?" (Matt. 18:21).

For Peter to propose forgiving someone up to seven times was a generous suggestion. According to a later rabbinic tradition, "If a man commits a transgression, the first, second and third time he is forgiven, the fourth time he is not."[16] Therefore, among Israel's spiritual leaders, forgiving someone three times was reasonable, but that was the limit. Peter is suggesting up to seven times, which not only is quantitative in nature, but also carries a qualitative nature as well. "Seven" symbolizes completeness in the biblical narrative. Therefore, it appears Peter is not just asking about a number, but more important, he's inquiring of what a complete or proper perspective on forgiveness entails.

This is why Jesus seizes the opportunity to expound on the nature of forgiveness by instructing, "I tell you, not seven times, but seventy-seven times" (Matt. 18:22).

At first read, Jesus' response appears to be random and embellished until you begin to recognize Jesus is employing a rabbinical teaching tactic known as *remez*. *Remez* is a Hebrew word meaning "hint." Often times, a rabbi would mention a keyword or phrase in his teaching that would "hint" at a passage from the Hebrew Scriptures (Old Testament) with the assumption the audience would know its broader meaning and context and import that context into the current teaching moment to add greater significance and clarity to the teaching.

Recently, there was a Capital One commercial where an army of Vikings came together to "stand against the tyranny of single mile credit cards." Alec Baldwin, the celebrity face of the company, jumps into the battle speech and offers his pitch for earning double miles with every purchase on the Venture card. The Vikings break out in exuberant applause at this life-changing news. Holding his smart phone, Baldwin asks the company's slogan question, "What's in your wallet?" Then almost as an aside, a Viking asks Baldwin, "Can you play games on that?" Baldwin immediately remarks while shaking his finger at the camera, "Not on the runway. No."

I fell off my couch laughing the first time I saw that commercial. If you're not aware, just prior to the release of that commercial, Baldwin got kicked off an American Airlines flight for refusing to shut off his phone during a delay on the runway. He wanted to continue playing his game (*Words with Friends*, for those of you who just have to know). Not only did Baldwin not extend an apology to American Airlines, but he went on *Saturday Night Live* that same week and performed a skit as the pilot of the flight, who issued "an apology to Mr. Alec Baldwin...an American treasure." It was a novel idea and, quite frankly, hilarious. It's why I found the commercial so amusing. Baldwin's last line was a *remez*. By referencing the runway incident, a different context was imported into the present moment, and it brought additional meaning to the commercial.[17]

This is what Jesus is doing when He references the number "seventy-seven." Showing up in only one place in the entire Hebrew Scriptures, Jesus takes Peter and His disciples back to a story in Genesis 4, where a man named Lamech is quoted as saying,

> "I have killed a man for wounding me,
>   a young man for injuring me.
> If Cain is avenged seven times,
>   then Lamech *seventy-seven* times." (vv. 23–24, emphasis mine)

Lamech was a descendant of Cain (the first murderer in the Bible). Although he demonstrates similar violent tendencies as his forefather, Lamech took his revenge to unprecedented levels. He went far beyond what was warranted or conceivable, and then boasted of his relentless passion for exacting this kind of limitless revenge, all reflected in the number "seventy-seven."

So when Jesus instructs His disciples to forgive someone "seventy-seven times," His *remez* pulls the Lamech story into the discussion, and Jesus' point becomes clear. He wants His followers to exemplify the same kind of relentless passion and thirst for forgiveness as Lamech did for vengeance. Just as Lamech was bent on exacting a revenge that was above and beyond the offense, Jesus wants His disciples to go above and beyond in forgiving the wrongs committed against them. To forgive "seventy-seven times" is Jesus' way of saying, "I want you to be endlessly forgiving others." For Jesus, this is to be a fundamental aspect of what it means to follow Him.

I don't know about you, but this feels a bit over the top. Living into a posture of endlessly forgiving others doesn't seem reasonable. What's more, forgiveness is excruciatingly difficult. And Jesus knew this. It's why He immediately launches into a parable to address the inherent reaction His hearers would have. Here's how the story begins:

> "Therefore, the kingdom of heaven is like a king who wanted to settle accounts with his servants. As he began the settlement, a man who owed him ten thousand bags of gold was brought to him. Since he was not able to pay, the master ordered that he and his wife and his children and all that he had be sold to repay the debt." (Matthew 18:23–25)

This is a story about extremes. "Ten thousand bags of gold" is an insurmountable debt. According to the scholarly estimations, a debt of this nature would have been at least two and a half billion dollars,[18] and would've taken a day laborer 164,000 years to repay![19] Any first-century listener would have gasped when they heard this.

It's why what happens next would have been even more shocking. For as Jesus continues:

> "At this the servant fell on his knees before him. 'Be patient with me,' he begged, 'and I will pay back everything.' The servant's master took pity on him, canceled the debt and let him go." (Matthew 18:26–27)

Clearly, it would've been impossible for the servant to repay such a debt. He and his family would be slaves for life. But in his desperation, he makes a promise to buy himself some time—a promise he knows he's unable to keep. Fully aware of the circumstances, the king, with unimaginable compassion and mercy, does the unthinkable. He forgives the debt, and the servant goes free. Absolutely breathtaking! Yet the story doesn't end here.

> "But when that servant went out, he found one of his fellow servants who owed him a hundred silver coins. He grabbed him and began to choke him. 'Pay back what you owe me!' he demanded. His fellow servant fell to his knees and begged him, 'Be patient with me, and I will pay it back.' But he refused. Instead, he went off and had the man thrown into prison until he could pay the debt." (Matthew 18:28–30)

The servant's response is preposterous, and is intended to elevate the blood pressures of the hearers. "A hundred silver coins" is roughly four thousand dollars.[20] The man has just been forgiven over two and a half billion dollars, and yet is unwilling to forgive another for a debt of four thousand. Can you imagine someone doing this? Jesus, knowing His audience is getting worked up, brilliantly correlates their emotions with those of the characters in the story by continuing with:

"When the other servants saw what had happened, they were out-raged and went and told their master everything that had happened. Then the master called the servant in. 'You wicked servant,' he said, 'I canceled all that debt of yours because you begged me to. Shouldn't you have had mercy on your fellow servant just as I had on you?' In anger his master handed him over to the jailers to be tor-tured, until he should pay back all he owed." (Matthew 18:31–34)

The servant doesn't get away with his merciless act. After betray-ing the grace of the king by his unwillingness to forgive another, the servant is confronted with the severity of his offense by being sent to jail and tortured. Justice has been served, and I imagine Jesus' disciples were thrilled with the end result. But knowing the teach-ing methods of their rabbi, Jesus doesn't tell the story to amuse His disciples. There's a purpose. In the event they haven't gotten it, Jesus concludes the parable by stating, "This is how my heavenly Father will treat each of you unless you forgive your brother or sister from your heart" (Matt. 18:35).

And the point of the parable is crystallized. God, as the king, in His great mercy and love, forgave each of us for an insurmountable debt. Irrespective of whatever is done to us, no one will ever owe us what we owed God. And God instructs us to forgive others with the same grace we were extended. When we fail to recognize how much we've been forgiven, we will struggle to forgive others. Jesus reminds us we are to be passionate about forgiving others because God has been passionate about forgiving us. To live a life of forgiving seventy-seven times, we must begin with an awareness of how much we've been forgiven.

According to Jesus, we forgive because we've been forgiven. Paul reminds followers of Jesus in Colossae about this when he writes,

"Bear with each other and forgive one another if any of you has a grievance against someone. Forgive as the Lord forgave you" (Col. 3:13). Paul takes the same approach with those residing in Ephesus and the surrounding region when he instructs, "Be kind and compassionate to one another, forgiving each other, just as in Christ God forgave you" (Eph. 4:32).

Foundational to forgiveness is an awareness of how we've been forgiven. The more we're able to grasp this, the more likely we'll be able to forgive others. But let's be honest. Jesus' teaching on forgiveness is still a hard one to swallow. Even if we know God has forgiven us extravagantly for our wrongs, it can be challenging to forgive others for theirs. People do some really nasty things. When we're the recipients of such evil, extending forgiveness can be gut-wrenching, if not seemingly impossible. And yet Jesus' contention is that it's not only possible, but absolutely necessary. Which may lead us to wonder if there's more to this conversation that would help us become people who are able to forgive seventy-seven times. The good news is, there is.

Nature of Forgiveness

In addition to consistently reminding ourselves of what God has done for us, it's imperative to have a proper understanding of forgiveness. I am convinced a major hurdle in being seventy-seven forgivers is that most of us don't understand the nature of forgiveness. Dr. Robert Enright has been researching and implementing forgiveness programs for more than twenty-five years. Touted as the unquestioned pioneer in the scientific study of forgiveness, and bearing the title "Father of Forgiveness Research," Enright has encountered thousands of situations where people have been wronged and are struggling to forgive.[21] Incredibly, he writes, "I've found that literally one hundred percent of the problems that people have with forgiveness are based on a misunderstanding of the concept."[22] If we're able to understand the nature of forgiveness, our ability to forgive others will be significantly enhanced.

Among the best books I've read in recent years is *As We Forgive* by Catherine Claire Larson. It was inspired by the award-winning documentary of the same name, and it recounts the stories of those who survived the 1994 Rwandan genocide, where an estimated 800,000 to a million people (300,000 were children) were slaughtered in a span of a hundred days by their own countrymen, and their journeys toward forgiveness and reconciliation. The stories seem to be an invention of fiction. They're so gruesome, it's hard to imagine human beings actually doing such things to one another. Here are people who have experienced the evilest of human horrors and yet they're forgiving their perpetrators. Their stories are some of the most compelling and hopeful stories of forgiveness I've ever come across. They have pushed me to be a better follower of Jesus in forgiving and loving others well. It was an awe-inspiring and transformational read, and one I read through tears.

What I found transformational was not only the stories themselves but also what came between the stories. Larson has what she calls "interlude chapters" thoughtfully placed between these stories of forgiveness. In these "interlude chapters," Larson tackles the various facets of forgiveness in order to give the reader a more proper understanding of the subject. What she presents isn't just theory. It's evidenced in the lives of these Rwandans, whose stories are being told in the adjacent pages. They gained a proper perspective on the nature of forgiveness. They had to. Their suffering was enslaving them, and they realized the only way to become free of this horrifying pain was to forgive their perpetrators. With a proper perspective, it became easier for them to forgive. Notice I didn't say it was easy for them to forgive. Forgiving this kind of evil isn't easy by any stretch of the imagination. But despite what they went through, forgiving their perpetrators became more accessible and possible based on an accurate understanding. If forgiveness is a possibility in their experience, it can be in ours as well.[23]

What Forgiveness Is Not

As we launch into the nature of forgiveness, it's most helpful to begin by naming what forgiveness is not.

Forgiveness is not condoning what happened. Forgiving someone is not saying what they did was okay, or it was a misunderstanding. It's not agreeing with it. It's not sweeping the situation under the rug or excusing it. And it's definitely not saying it didn't matter. In fact, the opposite is true. If something needs to be forgiven, it's significant enough to warrant forgiveness in the first place. Therefore, the need to forgive doesn't negate the importance of what happened. It affirms it.

Forgiveness is not forgetting what happened. There's a misconception that forgiveness entails both forgiving and forgetting. The Bible calls us to forgive. It never commands us to forget. That doesn't mean we hold the incident against someone, and keep reminding them of what they've done over and over again. But it does mean we don't become naïve to the fact it may happen again or that it happened in the first place. Forgiving your business partner who single-handedly derailed the business doesn't mean you get into another business venture with them. Forgiving your boyfriend for beating you doesn't mean you must stay in the relationship. Forgiving someone who verbally abused you doesn't mean you don't establish boundaries. In fact, in many cases it's absolutely necessary to put boundaries in place in order to protect yourself from letting that person harm you again. You can forgive them, but that doesn't mean things go back to the way they were. That relationship may never be the same again. That friendship may look entirely different from that point forward. And that's okay. Actions have consequences, and sometimes the broken-ness introduced into a relationship forever alters it.

Forgiveness is not always reconciling. Reconciliation is always the goal, but forgiveness isn't dependent upon reconciliation. Reconciliation requires two willing parties to address the brokenness of a situation. Therefore, it's a two-way street. Forgiveness is a one-way street. You can forgive someone irrespective of whether they want to be forgiven, believe they need to be forgiven, or even know they've been forgiven. Oftentimes, people have a hard time forgiving someone who's dead, because they've been told forgiveness means reconciling as well. That's not true. A woman who's tired of harboring bitterness toward her deceased father for abusing her when she was young can forgive him and move on. Forgiveness doesn't require a response from the other party. The decision to forgive is yours, and yours alone.

And forgiveness is not abolishing or forgoing legal ramifications, consequences, or reparations. If someone did something that requires some form of punishment, recompense, or legal action, forgiveness doesn't cancel this reality, nor should it. Sometimes people don't realize the harm they've done, or the seriousness of their offense, until justice has been levied against them. Oftentimes, people will not change until they've encountered an inciting incident that forces them to acknowledge their shortcomings or failures. As we've all likely experienced, our greatest blunders can serve as the greatest catalysts for growth and maturity. Therefore, just because you are willing to forgive your perpetrator doesn't mean you must rob them of their punishment, which could be instrumental in positively affecting their lives.

What Forgiveness Is

When Peter asks Jesus in Matthew 18:21 how many times he should forgive, the Greek word translated as "forgive" is *aphiēmi*, which literally means, "to release or set free."[24] When we read or hear such a definition, our inclination is to think we're talking about the person who did something to us. As if the one who hurt us is the one we need to set free. I believe that's part of it. But there's more to it. If you've been hurt by someone, and you're unwilling to forgive them, who's more hurt by your lack of forgiveness? You? Or them? For some of us, we have this notion if we don't forgive the one who hurt us, we're punishing them in some way. The truth is we're more affected by our lack of forgiveness than they are. So our actions don't make sense. As Anne Lamott puts it, "Not forgiving someone is like drinking rat poison and waiting for the rat to die."[25]

We often choose unforgiveness. It's our way of attempting to reestablish control of a situation that came about by something happening to us we couldn't initially control. But the irony is when we are unwilling to forgive someone, we allow them to have a controlling presence in our life, and in a sense, they own us. In our attempt to establish control, we actually allow the perpetrator to maintain control, and we're the ones who are enslaved and punished. The issue isn't them, it's us. Forgiveness is, first and foremost, about setting someone free, and then realizing all along it was you who was most in need of being set free. In setting yourself free, you set them free as well.

Forgiveness is letting go of our desire for revenge. It's giving up our plots to get even. It's no longer harboring a grudge against someone. It's letting go of our bitterness, anger, and rage. It's relinquishing our yearning for control. It's handing people over to God and trusting He will ultimately take care of it.

Forgiveness is a process. Just because we're supposed to forgive doesn't mean it's going to happen instantaneously or overnight. Forgiveness takes time. We can't rush the process or we may not truly forgive in the end. Depending on the offense, forgiveness may come rather quickly. Other times, forgiveness may take a while, and may only be possible after going through the healthy and necessary stages of grief. No one should be made to feel guilty for not being able to forgive right away. The journey toward forgiveness can be long and arduous.

Forgiveness is both reactive and proactive. We forgive in response to something that's done to us, and therefore it's reactive. But sometimes it needs to be proactive, which means forgiving in advance. I was recently talking to a friend who is in his fifties, and he told me that every time he spends time with his aging father, his father will say something to him that's hurtful. Although he limits the amount of time he spends with his toxic father, he still makes the effort to maintain a relationship. And because he knows his father is going to hurt him, he told me he must forgive him in advance for what he's going to do in order to be less affected by whatever painful words are spoken to him.

Forgiveness is painful. It will cost you something. Emotional pain doesn't dissipate over time. It either hibernates until an inopportune time, festers within our own soul, or gets passed on to others—generally the people we love the most. Pain cannot be left unaddressed. It must be dealt with, and the only way to strip it of its power is to absorb it. Forgiveness is difficult because in order to forgive, you must be willing to absorb the pain caused by another.

In fact, one of the Hebrew words that gets translated as "forgive" is *nasa*, which literally means, "to lift up, carry, take, or bear."[26] To forgive is to bear the weight and marks of the wrongs committed, without holding it against the one who committed them.

It Has a Source

Ed Dobson once said, "Forgiveness is a great idea, until you have someone to forgive, and then it's very difficult."[27] Agreed. That's why so many people prefer revenge. It's just easier. But anyone can do that. It takes great strength to forgive.

I don't know about you, but there are times when I don't have the strength to forgive. It's not that I'd rather enter into revenge. It's that I don't have what it takes to forgive. I may understand the nature of forgiveness, and be cognizant of how much God has forgiven me, but that doesn't mean I'm automatically able to forgive another. I struggle. Maybe you do, too. And yet Jesus still instructs us to forgive seventy-seven times. There's got to be another piece to the equation.

One of the most powerful moments in *As We Forgive* happens in a conversation between a woman named Chantel and a man named Pascal. Chantel is struggling to forgive a man named John who destroyed her family and her life. Her friend Pascal, who suffered similar horrors in the genocide, is doing everything in his power to assist her in her journey toward forgiveness. At one point, Chantel firmly says to Pascal, "I'm still not ready to forgive... [but] I do feel as if I'm moving closer to it. But still sometimes I feel helpless, especially when I think about the past."

In response, Pascal remarks, "I understand, of course. But I want you to know, forgiveness has a source. You can honestly say to God, 'I have no strength in me to forgive John. But you, O Lord, have the power to forgive. Give me the power to forgive him.' God will help you. I believe he will help you."[28]

Forgiveness has a source.

On our own strength, it's very difficult to forgive. Perhaps for some of us, the reason we've been having such difficulty forgiving is because we've been seeking to do it on our own strength. Pascal's words of wisdom to Chantal were not only insightful and helpful, but biblical. God is the God of all strength. And God is the source of all forgiveness. If we want to be people who are able to forgive seventy-seven times, then we need to be conduits through which the source of forgiveness can pass. We need the strength of Christ to flow through us if we're going to live out lives of forgiveness. And so we ask the God of forgiveness to resource us with His power to do for others what He has done for us.

Jesus once said, "By this everyone will know that you are my disciples, if you love one another" (John 13:35). We love God and we love others well when we forgive. Perhaps a defining characteristic of this love will be our scars. The work of forgiveness often leaves scars. But they are redemptive scars. They are scars that give witness to how God is working through us to bring restoration to our broken world. They are scars of victory. And they are scars that remind us we're doing for others what Christ has done for us. As Catherine Claire Larson so powerfully reminds us, "When God raised this man, Jesus Christ, from the dead, he didn't take away his scars. These scars testify to his pain, to his love, and to the extent to which God will go to conquer the evil of the world through the active suffering of forgiveness. Only through such active love can such scars of horror be transfigured into emblems of triumph."[29]

Samson missed out on his opportunity to have such scars. Jesus didn't. And neither should we. We're all going to be wronged. We're all going to get hurt. It's part of being human in a fallen world. But we don't have to play the part of the victim. We don't have to fall into the destructive cycle of vengeance. We can choose to forgive. We can choose to get right what Samson got wrong. With an awareness of what God has for us, a proper understanding of forgiveness, and the source of forgiveness coursing through us, we can choose to follow the way of Jesus and be the kind of people who forgive seventy-seven times.

CHAPTER 4

Scuffed Knees

The noise in the gym was deafening. I could feel my heart beating in my eardrums. The butterflies were desperately attempting to evacuate my chest. Butter-drenched popcorn mixed with the musty smell of sweaty basketball players. Raucous college students were jumping up and down. Everyone had been waiting for this game. There wasn't a single empty seat in the gym. Everywhere you looked there were people, their faces full of anticipation. Even though I'd been in similar environments during my high school career, the intensity of a game like this was significantly higher being a freshman on a collegiate basketball team.

We were midway through the season and playing our nonconference nemesis, located only four miles down the road in our great city of Grand Rapids, Michigan. It was technically an "away" game because we were playing at their gym. Despite their home court advantage, we were in control. We were off to the best start in school history, and we had been destroying teams. We were good.

We would go on to win the NAIA National Championship in an overtime thriller decided at the buzzer, becoming Cornerstone University's first basketball team to win it all, and in the process setting a single season school record of thirty-seven wins. Like I said, we were good. The problem was we knew it.

But back to the gym. It was an ugly game. That is, it was an ugly game for us. From the opening tip, we were pathetic. We missed several wide-open lay-ups, and countless free throws. We didn't dive for loose balls, or go after rebounds. We were lazy on offense, and lazy on defense. We got outworked in every aspect of the game. We didn't even put up a good fight. We thought we could just show up, and we were sorely mistaken. In front of several thousand people, we got humiliated. Two and a half hours prior we were soaring high, but as we sat in the locker room, our heads between our hands, we couldn't have been any lower.

The following day we arrived for practice to a nearly pitch-black gym. Someone had taken out a power line on the East Beltline and the athletic facility had lost power. From our perspective as players, this was divine intervention. God did love us and was looking out for our well-being. The punishment we knew we'd receive (and quite frankly, deserved) would simply have to wait another day, because clearly we couldn't practice in a gym with no lights.

I mentioned the gym was nearly pitch-black. By "nearly" I mean the exit signs above the doors provided just enough light to see the lines on the courts. You could hardly make out the baskets, so shooting was out of the question. And passing drills in the dark is a bad idea. No shooting. No passing. No lights. No practice. It was that simple.

Then a door swung open at the far end of the gym, and our coach walked across the floor. The darkness, however, did not hide the anger on his face. This was not a good omen. There was no exchange of greeting, only these now infamous words: "We don't need baskets or balls for what we're doing today."

I wanted to cry.

He instructed us to the baseline, and things went from bad to worse. We knew we were running sprints. The only question was, "How many?" In our wildest estimations, we couldn't have guessed the number of sprints. We ran and we ran and we ran. And then we ran some more. We ran until our legs practically fell off. It was awful. It was memorable. And that was the point. Our coach made sure that we wouldn't soon forget that pride was an unwelcome visitor.

Has your pride ever gotten the best of you?

Let's be clear. I'm not talking about the good kind of pride. There's good pride and there's bad pride. Good pride is the pride we can have in the school we went to, or in our place of work, or in how well our kids are doing, or in how great our lawn looks after spending hours mowing and trimming and weeding, and realizing we were so close to paying someone else to do it, but then being grateful we didn't because it was meaningful work.

Bad pride gives us an inflated view of ourselves. It comes with a false sense of security, and then painfully drops us in unwelcome places, such as in a locker room with our head between our hands, or wondering if our legs will ever work again after running them long past their functional threshold.

Has this kind of pride ever gotten the best of you?

Perhaps you were in school and had a significant test or exam, and you didn't put in the necessary time because you felt you didn't need to, and you ended up with a C or a D, or even worse, you failed.

Or maybe you were helping a friend move and you knew that box in the corner was too heavy, but you didn't want to appear weak so you didn't ask for help, and you ended up injuring your back.

Or worse, you were struggling in your marriage and refused

counseling because you thought you could figure it out on your own, and you found yourself in the kitchen with the divorce papers on the table awaiting your signature.

Or perhaps you were in a significant role of leadership and you cut some corners because you were convinced certain rules didn't apply to you, and you ended up losing your job and suffering public humiliation.

We've all had these kinds of experiences. Some of us are able to look back on them with humor. Others of us look back on them with sadness and a lingering sense of shame. Regardless of our perspective on the past, I'm willing to bet that we all resonate with the infamous and oft-quoted axiom "Pride goes before a fall."

This isn't just a nice, quotable saying like you might find in a fortune cookie. It's actually a shortened proverb that finds its roots in the wisdom literature of the Bible.

In Proverbs 16:18, we read, "Pride goes before destruction, a haughty spirit before a fall."

Like many proverbs and statements from the Hebrew Scriptures, it's a parallelism, which simply means a statement or idea is being repeated twice. "A haughty spirit before a fall" is another way of saying, "Pride goes before destruction." Hence, the proverb over time was simply shortened to "Pride goes before a fall."

Explore the key Hebrew words in the first line of this proverb and you'll start to get a pretty good picture of the nature of pride and how it works.

The word translated as "pride" is the Hebrew word *ga'on*. It comes from the verb *ga'a*, which means "to be high, to be tall, or to be majestic."[1] Pride carries the idea of towering or rising above everyone or everything else.

The word translated as "destruction" is the Hebrew word *shever*. *Shever* literally means "a breaking."[2]

So the idea being communicated in this proverb is that in our pride we become so high, so tall, so majestic as we tower above everyone and everything else that eventually we reach a height where we cannot sustain ourselves and we snap, and we break, and thus we fall.

If you're a parent, you've likely played with blocks with your kids. It happens all the time in our house. The kids get out the wooden blocks and immediately start putting one on top of another to see how high they can stack them. With a watchful eye, you notice they aren't stacking them perfectly atop one another, so you assist in realigning them. Ten blocks into the endeavor, the whole thing starts swaying back and forth, and your children inhale slowly with each successive placement. And then comes the moment when the tower of blocks reaches a height it can no longer support, and all the blocks come crashing down.

That's how pride works. Pride gives us an inflated view of ourselves and makes us believe we're tall and majestic, towering high above everyone and everything else. It makes us believe we're stable under our own strength and abilities. But it's a false sense of security, a foundation that sways back and forth, until eventually we break and everything comes crashing to the ground.

And it can be devastating.

Light and Dark

After a fleeting seven-day marriage that would make even Hollywood blush, and at least one recorded encounter with a prostitute, Samson appears to have found love. We're told in Judges 16 that Samson "fell in love with a woman in the Valley of Sorek whose name was Delilah" (v. 4).

The Sorek Valley is the valley Samson grew up next to and the valley in which Timnah lay—the same Timnah where Samson shredded the lion, burned up the crops with the jackals, and married his first wife. We don't know if this new woman is also from Timnah, if she is from Beth Shemesh, a city five miles up the valley to the southeast from Timnah and within eyeshot of Samson's hometown, or if she is from another city connected to the Philistines.

What we do know is she's not looking for love. She's looking for payment. She's been contracted by the Philistine leaders to discover the source of Samson's strength. Although it isn't specifically stated in the text, she is most certainly a Philistine. As the story unfolds, it becomes obvious why she was chosen. She's beautiful, charming, seductive, resourceful, intelligent, assertive, persistent, and most of all, motivated. And who wouldn't be motivated by sixteen and a half million dollars?

Nope, that's not a typo.

She is informed that a successful discovery of the source of Samson's strength and the subsequent action leading to his capture come with a payout of fifty-five hundred shekels of silver,[3] which is approximately sixteen and a half million dollars in today's economy![4]

That heightens the intensity of the story.

But it doesn't stop there, because we're also given her name—Delilah.

This is interesting because it's the first time we're given a woman's name in the Samson narrative. Prior to this point, every woman has been nameless, including Samson's mother, who is referenced nineteen times between Judges 13:2 and 14:9. In each instance she is referred to as either "Manoah's wife," "Samson's mother," or simply "the woman." Clearly, she's pivotal to the plot, but not important enough to be named.[5] In addition to this, we are not made privy to the name of Samson's first wife, her younger sister, or the prostitute in Gaza. And yet we're given Delilah's name.

As we explored earlier, names are very significant. A name is your identity and your destiny. Knowing the name of a character is a window into what their behavior is or ought to be. It's also a window into better understanding and anticipating the unfolding story.

Delilah is a name that packs a serious punch.

In Hebrew there is a linguistic connection and a pun between *Delilah* and *lilah*, which is the Hebrew word for "night."[6] The Hebrew word *de* means "of." Together, *Delilah* means "of the night."[7] And what comes with the night? Darkness.

If you don't recall, the meaning of Samson's name is "little sun" or "of the sun." And what comes with the sun? Light.

We are given Delilah's name because the writer wants us to know this is an epic showdown.

It is a showdown between "sun" and "night."

Between "light" and "darkness."

Between good and evil.[8]

Between an Israelite and a Philistine.

Between the legendary Samson and the seductive Delilah.

And as with any epic showdown, the stakes are immense.

Delilah doesn't waste any time and cuts to the chase. The first words from her mouth are, "Tell me the secret of your great strength and how you can be tied up and subdued" (Judg. 16:6).

Are you kidding me? That's her brilliant plan for getting him to disclose his secret? It's like an undercover detective walking up to a mob boss and saying, "Hello, I'm a cop, and I would like to join your organization so I can take note of everything you and your cronies are doing and then I would like to use all of that as evidence to put you and your entire organization behind bars for life without any chance for parole." And then concluding with, "I'm assuming you're okay with that?"

It's preposterous. But then again, Delilah has sixteen and a half million dollars on the line. So let's assume she knows what she's doing.

Samson finds this ruse rather amusing and decides to play a game of cat and mouse.[9] The game goes something like this: Samson tells Delilah that his strength would be sapped if something was specifically done to him—such as being tied up by seven fresh and undried bowstrings (cords made from the tendons of sheep or cows—again, violating the Nazirite vow of coming into contact with anything dead[10]), or being tied up with brand-new ropes, or if his hair was woven into a loom and tightened by a pin. Delilah will then act upon the disclosed information while having Philistine soldiers hidden in her room. Once her deed is completed, she'll announce to Samson that the Philistines are upon him. And given that the information Samson disclosed is full of lies, he'll effortlessly shake off the bindings and boldly display once again he's gotten the best of the Philistines.

Three rounds of this game are played before we're told that Delilah resorts to a different strategy. As the author records, "With such nagging she prodded him day after day until he was sick to death of it" (Judg. 16:16). This is brilliant. Even though Delilah is the villain in the story, you secretly want to applaud her ingenuity in employing a tactic that would make anyone miserable—a severe case of nagging. And it must have been some serious nagging because Samson does the unthinkable—he tells her everything, including the secret to his strength.[11]

Exhausted by the nagging and with his secret out in the open, Samson falls asleep on Delilah's lap. She sends word to her Philistine comrades, who silently enter the room, instruments in hand. With stealth and precision, they begin sheering the seven locks of Samson's hair until the mane of his strength has been completely removed. Once more, Delilah's voice rings with the alarming announcement, "The Philistines are upon you!" To which we are told, "He awoke from his sleep and thought, 'I'll go out as before and shake myself free.' But he did not know the LORD had left him" (Judg. 16:20).

Could there be a more devastating line than "He did not know the LORD had left him"? This is the writer's way of saying that his God-given gift was no longer able to save him.

They then gouge out his eyes and haul him off in chains to Gaza, the most significant of the Philistine cities. Delilah gets paid, and the reality is painfully clear. The "darkness" overcame the "light" as the "sun" was eclipsed by the "night."

What a baffling story. Think about the details. Everything from Delilah being so blunt about her intentions, to Samson seeing the entire scheme being played out on three separate occasions, to Samson telling his secret, and then to his being shocked by the end results.

It makes you wonder how someone could be so dim-witted, act so illogically, and be that naïve?

In a word—pride.

Pride makes us delusional. The higher we get, the more detached from reality we become, and our pride overshadows any logic or sensibility, resulting in decisions that are deeply irrational.

Samson had a "high" view of his positional status, his skills, and his ability to control a situation. His pride made him feel unconquerable. He treats his relationship with Delilah as one big game. He is apathetic and does what he wants because he believes the rules don't apply to him.

And this isn't the first episode where we see him fall victim to his pride. We see it in his demanding to have the Philistine woman of Timnah, violating both family values and God's command to refrain from marrying foreign women. We see it in his smug offering of a riddle that boasts of his lion killing and offends and shames the hosts of the wedding festival. We see it in his carrying of the Gaza gate to the highest point in southern Israel, an arrogant demonstration of his greatness and domination of the Philistine people. We see it in his constant and effortless disregard of his Nazirite vow. We see the evidence of his pride over and over again, and remarkably this story with Delilah won't be the last time we'll see it. But it's in this episode where he reaches a height he can no longer sustain and he snaps, and breaks, and crashes hard to the ground. For as the well-known saying goes, "The bigger they are, the harder they fall."

We see this all the time.

Open any newspaper or watch any news program and pride is at the core of many headlines. On a weekly basis, we hear about famous athletes, Hall of Fame coaches, movie stars, prominent politicians, school board officials, CEOs, and others whose prideful actions led to a loud and painful collapse.[12]

The truth of the matter is that pride isn't something that just surfaces in the sports arenas, or in Hollywood, or in Washington political offices, or in businesses on Wall Street. It shows up in our own jobs, in our own schools, in our churches, in our own homes, and in our own hearts. Pride appeals to us all. It's everywhere, and it's lethal.

Pride Seeks Gaps

Sometimes pride is easy to identify. But often it's difficult to spot because we don't understand pride's underlying agenda and the way it gets fleshed out in our lives. Pride isn't just about making us tall—height is only a means to an end. Pride's goal is creating gaps.

When our local rival trounced our basketball team, it wasn't simply that we saw ourselves as being tall; it was that we saw ourselves as being taller than them. In our minds, there was a gap. There was a gap between our ability to control the outcome of the game and their ability to do the same. When Samson was toying with Delilah, there was a gap in his mind between his ability to control the situation and Delilah's.

In both situations, a gap was present because the primary party saw themselves at a different level than the opposing party. If we had viewed our nemesis to be of identical height, there would have been no gap for pride to reside in. If Samson had viewed Delilah as an equal, he wouldn't have acted with such arrogance.

This is often how pride manifests itself. It creates a gap between how we view ourselves and how we view others in relation to ourselves, and the gap can be ugly. As Jeff Cook, a pastor, author, and philosophy professor at the University of Northern Colorado, defines it, "Pride is the natural love for myself magnified and perverted into disdain for others."[13] Jesus illustrated this in a story about a Pharisee and a tax collector who went up to the temple to pray. In striking contrast to the prayer of the tax collector, the prayer on the lips of the Pharisee went like this, "God, I thank you that I am not like other people—robbers, evildoers, adulterers—or even like this tax collector" (Luke 18:11). When gaps like this exist, all sorts of destructive behaviors begin to fester and grow.

This is why we get so angry when other drivers on the road aren't performing to our perceived level of competency. We are the standard for driving proficiency and their performance has clearly exposed a gap between our standard and their execution, and that irritates us.

Pride can begin subtly. When we meet someone, we often use the language of "sizing them up." We don't necessarily care about who they are as a person. We simply want to know how they compare to us. So we ask questions about what they do and where they went to school and then bend the conversation so we discuss the kind of car they drive or what neighborhood they live in, all the while trying to gauge their "height." If they're taller than us, we begin plotting and scheming all the ways they can assist or improve our height and status. But if they're "shorter" than us, we beam with satisfaction in the gap that exits and then often "look down" upon the individual who doesn't have the same level of education or job or club membership we have.

It's why we'll often make derogatory comments toward others. When we see ourselves at a certain "height" and someone we perceive to be "below" us begins to get "taller" and therefore closes the gap, we'll often say something that is downright cruel and discouraging. We use the language of "cutting them down" because that's exactly what we're attempting to do. We're trying to cut down their height so we can protect the gap our pride has created, and we often defend it at all costs.

There are gaps between how we view ourselves in relation to others. Then there's the gap between perception and reality.

Think about the couple who get a divorce and you're shocked by the news. From the outside everything looked like it was going well. But the news of the divorce exposed the presence of a gap. There was a gap between what that couple wanted you to believe was happening and what was actually going on in their marriage.

Think about the person who's addicted to pornography, alcohol, drugs, food, shopping, or something no one wants to acknowledge—busyness. It's destroying them, yet they refuse to openly share it because telling the truth would expose a gap between what others believe to be true about them and what is actually going on in their life. The fear and embarrassment is just too much. Or they may simply be in denial, which is a form of pride, since denial is not coming to terms with reality and maintaining a gap between reality and what one wants to believe to be true.[14]

Think about the person who never answers a question with, "I don't know." They're very intelligent, and likely find their identity in what they know. When someone asks a question they don't know the answer to, they'll lie or give a fluff answer because they don't want to expose a gap between what someone thinks they know and what they may actually know about that particular question or subject.

I struggled with this a lot as a young preacher. I began preaching at the age of twenty-five during my first year of seminary. Being considerably younger than the majority of the seven-hundred-member congregation I was regularly teaching, I desperately sought to establish myself as a teacher worth listening to, and not someone simply to be endured. It didn't help my cause one Sunday when a gentleman approached after the second service and remarked, "You'll be a better teacher when you've had more life experience." Ouch. That one hurt. Granted, I knew what he was getting at, and there was truth in his critique. But all I heard was, "You're too young right now. Only when you get older will you have something to say."

I responded by having an answer for everything. I thought if I had an answer for everything, everyone would respect me. Using the words "I don't know" would expose a gap in my knowledge base, and whatever respect a questioner had for me would be compromised— at least that's what I believed. So I stayed away from those words.

Although I still struggle with this at times, it has taken me several years to realize that people actually respect you more when you can acknowledge what you don't know. It makes you human. What's more, it validates the answers to questions you do know, which gives you more authority—the very thing you were seeking all along.

Gaps come in all shapes and sizes, and the culprit is pride because that's what it does. Pride will do anything and everything to create, maintain, or expand gaps because with the presence of gaps comes security—a belief that we are in control. Pride makes us feel secure, and the larger the gap, the more secure we feel. And since we are gluttons for security, pride will do anything to maintain or create gaps.

The irony is that these very gaps become our undoing. When our pride gets the best of us, it's because the gap has become so great that it can no longer sustain us. We thought the gap was our security, but it was actually our weakness. That's why we break, and snap, and engage in all sorts of destructive behaviors, and it's ultimately why things will eventually come crashing to the ground. It's just a matter of time.

Getting Low

We must combat the deadly nature of pride. We must deal with our propensity to want to be tall, and address the gaps that appear and expand in our lives. In order to do so, it's helpful to begin with the apostle Paul.

In Romans 12, he writes to a community of Jesus' followers, "For by the grace given me I say to every one of you: Do not think of yourself more *highly* than you ought, but rather think of yourself with sober judgment, in accordance with the faith God has distributed to each of you" (v. 3, emphasis mine). Did you notice the language of "height"? Paul is alluding to pride here, and he is pleading with his audience to refrain from getting too tall. In order to do so, his recommendation is to view oneself with "sober judgment." The phrase "sober judgment" is the Greek word *sōphronein* and it means "to be in a right mind,"[15] which carries the idea of having a proper perspective or knowing one's proper place in the world.

To have a proper perspective or to know one's proper place in the world is to essentially know how to interact within our world. Paul specifically addresses this in his letter to the Philippians. In Chapter 2, he writes, "Do nothing out of selfish ambition or vain conceit. Rather, in humility value others *above* yourselves, not looking to your own interests but each of you to the interests of the others" (vv. 3–4, emphasis mine). Again, notice the language associated with "height." The word "above" comes in connection with the word "humility." The Greek word for "humility" here is *tapeinophrosunē* (try saying that ten times fast) and it literally means "lowliness of mind." If we look at the verb form connected to this word, a more helpful picture emerges. That Greek word is *tapeinoō*, and it means "to get low."[16]

It makes sense. If pride's goal is to puff us up, make us tall, and create gaps in our lives, the best way to combat it is by deliberately getting low. When we do so, we close the gaps pride creates, because humility is a gap destroyer. Or for you Superman fans, humility is pride's kryptonite.

For some of us, we hear the word "humility" and think, "Seriously, Paul, that's the best you could come up with?" It's almost as if "humility" gives us a knee-jerk reaction. The reason is that biblical humility is notoriously misunderstood.

In a brilliant article on the virtue of humility, the late Dwight Pryor captured a common view of the humble when he wrote, "In our ego-centric, power-driven culture, the humble typically are depicted as wimpy, wishy-washy and weak. They are ineffectual persons, often with feelings of inadequacy."[17]

It's commonly held that the essence of humility is downplaying whatever skills or talents one has or successes one has achieved. It's as if openly acknowledging one's gifts and achievements is a violation of humility. Therefore, we typically associate humility with a poor self-image, or at least the appearance of a poor self-image. The problem, however, is that when we operate within these so-called confines of humility, we exhibit a false piety. And as Pryor notes, "The false piety fostered by a poor self-image is not biblical humility. In truth, an inadequate self-image is the same coin as an inflated self-image, just the reverse side. And the coin is 'self.' "[18]

I had to reread that last statement several times in order to let it sink in and to fully appreciate it. What Pryor is conveying is that when we exhibit a false piety, the focus is on ourselves. The irony is that in doing so, we do not embody humility, but pride—because at the heart of pride is a focus upon self. So in our attempt to steer clear of pride, we actually become what we're trying to avoid.

This way of understanding pride is missing something. It's why Pryor goes on to define humility in this way: "True humility is not thinking less *of* yourself, just thinking less *about* yourself—because the currency of your life is God, not self. Your desire is for God to be all in all, for His kingship to advance and His name to be sanctified in the world."[19]

His point is that true humility recognizes what our proper place is and acts accordingly—which is precisely Paul's point in Romans 12 when he admonishes the Roman believers to battle pride with "sober judgment." We are servants to the King and whatever gifts and resources we have been given are to be used for God's purposes and glory. So when someone acknowledges a gift or talent you have, own it. Don't think less of yourself. Own up to the reality that God has given you a gift or has blessed you with certain resources, and find a way to acknowledge God in the process.[20] By downplaying the gifts you've been given, you are stripping God of the glory due Him because God is the one who gave you that gift. By denying the gift, you are denying God.

In the same breath, we must recognize that by owning up to the gift, we do so with the understanding that we are called to use that gift on behalf of God for the sake of others. It's never about us. It's about God, and God's desire is that we use our gifts and resources to join Him in what He is doing in the world to bring restoration and wholeness to every arena of life. This is why pride has no place in the Kingdom of God, because pride makes it about me. But humility is about others, making it the antithesis of pride. Hence, true humility is not thinking less of ourselves, just thinking less about ourselves, and orienting our focus to God and others.

Bend a Knee

If pride is about being tall and focusing on ourselves, and humility is about getting low and focusing on others, then what does humility look like in everyday flesh-and-blood life?

As we've seen, the Hebrew language is visually rich, meaning the words themselves communicate an image—a picture. The Hebrew verb *barakh* is particularly fascinating in this regard. *Barakh* is often translated in the English as "to bless" or "to praise," but its literal meaning is "to bend a knee."[21]

How are blessing and praising connected to the bending of a knee?

I'm taller than my wife—not by much, but noticeably so. If she and I were to stand side by side and I were to ask you, "Who's taller?" you would naturally respond, "You are." But what if I got down on one knee and then asked you, "Who's taller?" Your immediate response would be, "She is." What did I do? I bent the knee, and in doing so, I made my wife taller. And that's precisely the word picture *barakh* is communicating. To praise or to bless someone is to bend the knee in order to make them taller or bigger.[22]

Let's take this further.

What happens when you bend the knee is you get lower to the ground. And the word for getting low is "humility." Paul speaks about humility in Philippians 2 by saying that in our humility we would value others *above* ourselves, and that we would not look to our own interests but to the interests of others. When we bend the knee, we enter a posture where we're literally valuing others "above" ourselves, and we do so with the intention of shifting the focus from ourselves to them. Furthermore, in our willingness to become low, we demonstrate that our desire is to bless and praise them by serving their interests. Therefore, the essence of humility is service.

Perhaps that's worth repeating. The essence of humility is service.

Followers of God are called to a life of service because they are called to a life of humility.

And no one has embodied this reality better than Jesus Christ. Perhaps this is why Paul continues his section on humility in his letter to the Philippians with these words: "In your relationships with one another, have the same mindset as Christ Jesus: Who, being in very nature God, did not consider equality with God something to be used to his own advantage; rather, he made himself nothing by taking the very nature of a servant, being made in human likeness. And being found in appearance as a man, he humbled himself by becoming obedient to death—even death on a cross!" (Phil. 2:5–8).

This is absolutely staggering.

In the ancient world, everything was about making oneself big. Pharaohs, kings, emperors, and other political leaders wanted everyone to know they were large and in charge. So they constructed big buildings and had giant sculptures made of themselves and had scribes write documents about how great and powerful and successful they were—all for the prideful purpose of making themselves appear as big as possible.

But Jesus is doing the very opposite.

Notice again these phrases:

"did not consider equality with God something to be used to his own advantage"

"made himself nothing"

"taking the very nature of a servant"

"humbled himself"

For Jesus, the incarnation was not about becoming big. It was about becoming small. This is what makes the incarnation so astounding—the big becomes small, the high becomes low, the God of the universe sheds His glory in order to squeeze into human skin.

No wonder it threw everyone off when the Savior of the world arrived as a baby in a manger to a poor teenage couple in the presence of lowly shepherds. No wonder it was perplexing for many as

He continued to live a life of humble means until He was humiliated on a cross. Jesus never sought to make Himself great; He sought to make Himself small, and that kind of behavior was unexpected in the consciousness of the ancient world. But Jesus didn't come to adhere to the patterns of the world; Jesus came to fundamentally change the world. And He did so by serving it, which was the intention all along. For as Jesus revealed to His disciples, "The Son of Man did not come to be served, but to serve, and to give his life as a ransom for many" (Mark 10:45).[23]

Jesus is the quintessential example of having every right to be "high" and yet becoming "low." Jesus had every right to demand that humanity serve Him, and yet He does the very opposite—He serves humanity. Jesus didn't come so that the knee could be bent to Him. Jesus came in order to bend the knee to humanity. Over and over and over again, Jesus is setting an example for His disciples to follow.

Besides his sacrificial death, nowhere is this example more evident than in Jesus' hours before his arrest, which would forever be etched on the hearts of his disciples. In John 13, we read about their final meal together. He has been eagerly awaiting this Passover meal. For over three years, Jesus has been a father to these young men, pouring His soul into them.[24] They were His boys, and everything Jesus did in his ministry was for the purpose of training and equipping them to be an extension of Himself so they could carry on the mission of God in the world. And now the time is up. This is His last meal with them and His last opportunity to give them one last teaching that will encompass the purpose of their training and the essence of His presence on earth.

Like all great teachers, Jesus doesn't instruct them only with words, He demonstrates with action. Rising from the cushion of this reclining meal, Jesus stands in the presence of His disciples, removes His outer cloak, and with a towel and water basin in hand, He does the unthinkable. He stoops down, bends a knee, and one by one He washes their feet.

If you scan the annals of ancient customs, you'll be hard pressed to find an action any lower than this. Loosing someone's sandals and then personally washing their feet was the most servile of tasks, reserved for the lowest of society. And even though Judaism stressed a life of humility, it upheld strict societal roles, in which under no circumstances would someone of Jesus' status do something this appalling.[25] Jesus shattered any social hierarchy with this shocking act.

And the disciples are astounded and perplexed, particularly the captain of the crew, Peter, who openly objects to Jesus with the emphatic, "You shall never wash my feet." To which Jesus responds, "Unless I wash you, you have no part in me" (John 13:8). It's as if Jesus says to Peter, "You've got to feel it. You've got to experience it. You've got to fully embrace what I am doing, because until you do, you won't reach out to others to this extent. This is who I am. This is why I came, and this is what I am calling you to do, because it is this kind of sacrificial service that will change the world."

And then just in case the weight of the moment wasn't fully felt or understood by all of his disciples, Jesus concludes the washing of their feet with these words:

"Do you understand what I have done for you? You call me 'Teacher' and 'Lord,' and rightly so, for that is what I am. Now that I, your Lord and Teacher, have washed your feet, you also should wash one another's feet. I have set you an example that you should do as I have done for you. Very truly I tell you, no servant is greater than his master, nor is a messenger greater than the one who sent him. Now that you know these things, you will be blessed if you do them." (John 13:12–17)

Jesus bent a knee to us all. He set an example of the most compelling nature, because He wanted to compel us with His love and service. And Jesus' desire is that we'd jump at every opportunity to bend a knee and do the same. Our proper place in the world is on a knee. And it's on our knee where we experience our full humanity, and what it means to live. This is the example Jesus set. This is the model we're to follow.

So the question we must wrestle with is, "Who bends the knee to whom?"

Who bends the knee to whom in your world?

Who bends the knee to whom in your workplace?

Who bends the knee to whom in your school?

Who bends the knee to whom in your friendships?

Who bends the knee to whom in your family?

Who bends the knee to whom in your marriage?

It's six o'clock in the evening. You're coming home from work and you're exhausted. It's been a long day and all you want to do is kick up your feet and rest. Your spouse has had a long day as well. Perhaps they've been home all day with the kids or are arriving home at the same time after picking them up from day care. In that moment, who bends the knee to whom? Do you bend the knee to your spouse, or do you expect your spouse to bend the knee to you?

Since I'm a husband, let me briefly address the husbands. Fellas, when you asked your wife to marry you, I'm guessing you got down on one knee in order to pop the question—you bent the knee. Do you still bend the knee today?

Jesus was a knee bender. He had scuffed knees from all the knee bending He did. Do we have scuffed knees from doing the same? Or do we expect the knee to be bent to us? If we expect the knee to be bent to us, we will be nothing like Jesus. But if we're willing to shift our focus and get low, bending a knee can change everything.

If you want to save your marriage...bend a knee.

If you want to strengthen your marriage...bend a knee.

If you want to improve your relationship with your child...bend a knee.

If you want to deepen your friendship...bend a knee.

If you want to impact your school...bend a knee.

If you want to improve your sports team...bend a knee.

If you want to make a difference at your job...bend a knee.

If you want to strengthen your church...bend a knee.

If you want to demonstrate Jesus to the world...bend a knee.

If you want to change this world, then do what Jesus did...and bend a knee.

Bending a knee is hard to do, I know. Even though I'm a pastor, a husband, and a father, I struggle with bending a knee to others. I want others to bend a knee to me. I want them to serve my needs. I want them to make me tall. Bending to others takes effort. It expends energy. It's inconvenient, and it often goes against every impulse in our bodies. But it's the difficulty that affirms the importance. Perhaps this is why Jesus says to his disciples, "The greatest among you is the one who is willing to serve."[26] It takes great strength to bend a knee. This is why the humble are not weak—they are very, very strong. And according to Jesus, bending a knee and serving others is the most compelling thing we can do.

This is why the story of Samson feels so empty and isn't compelling. There isn't a single reference in the entire narrative of Samson serving someone other than himself. Samson bends a knee to no one. He doesn't bend a knee to his parents, his wife, or the people. He doesn't even bend a knee to God. He is the quintessential example of pride, and pride bends a knee to no one. Because when we see ourselves high and lifted up, majestic[27] and towering above everyone else, we believe the knee is to be bent to us. Pride does not serve. Pride expects to be served.

Samson embodied pride.

Jesus embodied humility.

Samson sought to be tall.

Jesus sought to be small.

Samson ended up breaking.

Jesus ended up exalted.

Listen to how Paul concludes his section on humility in his letter to the Philippians:

> Therefore God exalted him [Jesus] to the highest place and gave him the name that is above every name, that at the name of Jesus every knee should bow, in heaven and on earth and under the earth, and every tongue acknowledge that Jesus Christ is Lord, to the glory of God the Father. (2:9–11)

In the ancient world, you gained your authority by demonstrating the power you had to make others serve you. But Jesus gains His authority by serving us. The reason every knee will bow and every tongue will confess is because Jesus served. Jesus was not about power plays, manipulation, coercion, or making someone submit through fear. His goal was to compel us to follow. The greatest became the least so that humanity could be served, and in the process Jesus became tall. Which is true for us as well. In the words of Jesus, "Those who exalt themselves will be humbled, and those who humble themselves will be exalted" (Matt. 23:12).

Pride says it's about being high.

Humility says it's about being low.

Pride says it's about widening the gap.

Humility says it's about closing the gap.

Pride says it's all about me.

Humility says it's about bending a knee.

Samson got it wrong.

Jesus got it right.

Whose example will you follow?

CHAPTER 5

Designed for Struggle

I met Jay a few months after graduating from college. He was working as a medical rep out of Fort Wayne, Indiana, and his boss had partnered with my father on a project. Through this project, my father met Jay and intuitively sensed we'd be great friends if only we met. He was right. The moment I met Jay, it was like reuniting with a long-lost brother.

Two months into this friendship, Jay began talking about a large group of friends getting together for a party in six weeks. It was going to take place at Bethel College in Mishawaka, Indiana, where his fiancée was a senior, and where he had recently graduated. Apparently, there were going to be a number of people there Jay wanted me to meet. At least that's the story he wanted me to believe.

Over the next several weeks, I received multiple calls from Jay indicating that the large group gathering was dwindling due to a number of unexpected reasons. Although the reasons were legitimate, the frequency of his calls should have tipped me off that he was up to something. Still, we hadn't been friends for very long so I didn't think anything of it.

The weekend of the party arrived, and Jay had a surprise for me.

He was taking me to a Notre Dame football game in South Bend. Since it was an early afternoon game, and the stadium was only fifteen minutes away from the party, which was slated to begin at six, we had plenty of time to soak in the renowned Irish experience. What a friend! And what a surprise!

But that wasn't the only surprise. Taking advantage of my excitement and appreciation for his generosity, Jay informed me there wasn't a group gathering that evening. There was no party. There never had been. The whole thing had been a setup.

Uncertain about my friend's intentions, and even more confused by his devious smile, I listened as he revealed his evil plan—a double date. "Is this a joke?" It wasn't. It was a double date with his fiancée, Erica, and her roommate, whom I had never met and knew nothing about. I'd been set up—a blind date, without my consent, and only a few hours' notice. I guess it could have been worse. At least I got a football game out of it.

Don't get me wrong. I jokingly call his plan "evil," but it was actually quite amusing. I don't normally get duped, and I was impressed by his ability to pull off such a clever endeavor. However, I wasn't thrilled about it either. Seven months prior I had broken off an engagement just three months before the wedding. It was one of the most depressing times of my life, and it left me with little desire to date anyone seriously for some time.

But all that changed on that Saturday in mid-October. A poet once wrote, "Life is queer with its twists and turns," and I found this to be true. It was a date I hadn't asked for and didn't want. And yet it was a date that would change my life forever. Exactly eleven months later, Shallon and I were married outside my parents' house on a picturesque Saturday afternoon, in front of several hundred friends and family. It couldn't have been more glorious.

It sounds a bit like destiny, doesn't it? Like the stars aligned for our encounter. And you're probably expecting me to mention how we completed each other, and the honeymoon lasted five years, and we lived in a perfect home, in a perfect neighborhood, and it never snowed at our house, even though we lived in Michigan!

Not. Even. Close.

It was awful.

Especially that first year. Granted, many couples have a rough first year. But to say we had a rough year would be like saying the President doesn't wield much power, or fire isn't all that hot. It's a drastic understatement. At times, we couldn't get along to save our lives. We'd ebb and flow between good times and I-can't-believe-I-married-this-person times.

Did I mention it was awful?

I distinctly remember sitting on the floor one evening in our living room during one of our life-sapping arguments. Exhausted and frustrated, and feeling utterly helpless, I slammed my right fist into the floor. The pain shot through my hand like an electrical current. For the next twelve months I was unable to shake anyone's hand without feeling like I was going to pass out. Never mind the fact that my dad was a renowned physical therapist. I wasn't going to have him diagnose my hand because generally the question gets asked, "How did you do this?" Consequently, I relegated my hand to being collateral damage in this unfolding saga.

Things got so bad I would get up in the middle of the night to use the bathroom, and my wife would ask me where I was going. It didn't matter if it was midnight or 3 a.m., she was awake. It was as if her body triggered a wake-up call when my bladder had reached capacity. She was convinced I was leaving her, and would do so in the middle of the night. For months my wife lay four feet away (because

I literally slept on the edge of our bed) wondering when I was going to leave. For months I lay there wondering how badly I had messed up my life by marrying this woman.

Never in my life had I felt so alone.

I was scared. I was confused. And yes, I was despairing of the situation. But what surprised me most was how lonely I felt. It was crippling. It was for her, too. Like two ships sailing parallel in the night, we knew the other was around, but it felt like we were navigating the dark waters alone.

It's kind of ironic. We tend to think of loneliness in the context of being alone. But as we were painfully learning, marriage doesn't eliminate loneliness. It gains access to the individual as well as to the couple. Not only did my wife and I experience loneliness in our marriage, but we experienced marriage as loneliness.

Nobody knew our marriage was a mess. We didn't want anyone to know the problems we had or what was happening in the confines of our home. So we told no one. Not our families. Not our pastor. Not even our best friends. In the process of keeping silent, we isolated ourselves from others. We were alone, and for some reason we were content to keep it that way.

Clearly this wasn't how two people were designed to journey together.

Not Good

I am convinced that all of life's great lessons have their origin in the first three chapters of Genesis. Seriously, they're all there. One such lesson makes its first appearance in Genesis 2. But as with all great stories, we must understand the movement leading up to the moment. So let's briefly review Genesis 1.

In Genesis 1, God is creating the world. He is creating planets, and palm trees, and porcupines, and funky little fish that puff up when scared, and people. It's a beautiful and vibrant world, full of potential and possibility. And it's a world the Creator seems thoroughly delighted with. We see this stamp of approval rhythmically placed in the cadence of the Genesis 1 creation account.

Verse 4   And God saw that the light was good.
Verse 10   And God saw that it was good.
Verse 12   And God saw that it was good.
Verse 18   And God saw that it was good.
Verse 21   And God saw that it was good.
Verse 25   And God saw that it was good.
Verse 31   And God saw all that he had made, and it was very good.

Seven times in this opening chapter, God emphatically confirms His profound sense of delight and goodness with creation. And then we come to Genesis 2, another creation account. Or more accurately, it's a more focused account of what transpired in the creation of the man and woman. Adam is created first from the dust of the earth. He is then placed in the Garden of Eden, a beautiful, sinless environment, where he is given the task of stewarding the garden. Eve has yet to be created, and Adam is enjoying a pure, unadulterated relationship with the living God. It's precisely at this moment that God states, "It is not good for the man to be alone. I will make a helper suitable for him" (Gen. 2:18).

What?

"It is *not* good."

I was under the impression everything God had created was good.

It's like this statement chose to drive the wrong way on a one-way street, or show up at a swim meet in a clown suit. It's totally out of place.

Additionally, God mentions that Adam is alone. But he isn't. God is there with him. It's a perplexing statement until we recognize that God is making an earth-shattering point about the limitation He included in the relational design between Himself and humanity. And the point is this: God is not enough for us!

Let that sink in for a moment.

God purposely created the world to function in such a way that He is not enough for us. This is why God says, "It is not good for the man to be alone." If God were all that Adam needed, then Adam would not be alone. But he is alone. Not because God is there, but because one of his kind is not. By choice, God limited His ability to be everything Adam needed.

This flies in the face of what many of us have heard. On a regular basis, I hear people say, "All you need is God. God is enough." Well, that sounds nice, but the problem is that it isn't true, or even biblical for that matter, from a relationship point of view. If we're talking about grace, then these statements are true. God's grace is enough. However, if we're talking about relationships, they're not.

Does God desire that we devote every aspect of our lives to Him? Absolutely. Does God desire to walk with us and bring us into a deeper understanding of Himself? Without question. So please understand, I'm not downplaying the need for God here. I'm elevating the need for others, which is precisely what God is doing in this Genesis passage.

We were designed for human companionship. We were not designed to walk alone. Archbishop Desmond Tutu once asserted, "A self-sufficient human being is sub-human...God has made us so that we will need each other."[1] Life was never intended to be just a me-and-God thing. According to God, this "is not good." We were created to journey through life in community with other human beings. It's in the fabric of our DNA.

In Genesis 1, we read, "God created mankind in his own image, in the image of God he created them; male and female he created them" (v. 27). Astounding! The living God of the universe stamps His image into the makeup of humanity. As humans, we bear the image of God, and thus reflect the nature of God.

A fundamental and distinct belief of the Christian faith, known as the Trinity, is that God consists of three members (Father, Son, and Holy Spirit). So it's one God, but three members, functioning as a single unit. Therefore, the essence of God's existence and functionality is rooted in community. God is a community unto Godself (there's some good theological language for you). To be made in God's image is to reflect the communal nature of God. We are communal beings, and have been designed to journey in community with others. This is what God purposed His created beings to do. Indeed, this is good.

Samson's a Lone Ranger

As I've read the Samson story, I've been struck by the individual nature of the narrative. What initially caught my attention was what happens when Samson shows up for his wedding in Judges 14. Notice how the narrator records it: "And there Samson held a feast, as was customary for young men. When the people saw him, they chose thirty men to be his companions" (vv. 10–11).

There's a lot of scholarly debate about who these thirty men are, how they were chosen, and what purpose they served.[2] And the discussion among scholars is valid. What's interesting to me is that Samson shows up to his wedding alone. He has no friends with him. He has no companions of his own. His groomsmen have to be provided for him.

At first, this just seems peculiar. But the more you read the

Samson narrative, the more you come to realize this is par for the course for Samson. Samson is a lone ranger. His story is one lone action after another. Notice the storyline.

He sees the Philistine woman in Timnah alone.

He attacks and kills the lion alone.

He retrieves honey from the lion's carcass alone.

He arrives at his wedding alone.

He strikes down thirty men in Ashkelon alone.

He catches three hundred jackals alone.

He burns the summer and winter crops in the Sorek Valley alone.

He attacks an unidentified number of Philistines alone.

He flees to the cave in the rock of Etam alone.

He strikes down one thousand Philistines near Lehi alone.

He hauls the Gaza gate to the region of Hebron alone.

He is subdued by Delilah and the Philistines alone.

He grinds grain in prison alone.

He brings down the Dagon temple alone.

Everything Samson does, he does alone. He journeys with no one. Granted, you could refute this with the three women we encounter in his story. But truth be told, those relationships appear to be based on lust rather than love. And the only mention of anyone connected to Samson, other than his parents (in reference to the wedding), comes after Samson dies. We're told, "His brothers and his father's whole family went down to get him. They brought him back and buried him between Zorah and Eshtaol in the tomb of Manoah his father" (Judg. 16:31).

That's it. Four chapters of Samson, and Samson alone. In short, he lives alone, struggles alone, and dies alone. As a Nazirite called to reflect God's desire for how to live, Samson didn't grasp the importance and fundamental need of journeying with others. But neither did my wife and I. We didn't understand our need to journey with others. We did what Samson did. We were lone rangers, and it almost destroyed us. The only difference was we began to understand the importance of journeying with others before it was too late.

Helper Suitable

If we are communal beings, and God's desire is that we journey through life with others, the question becomes, "How are we to journey together?" That's precisely what's addressed in the second half of the Genesis 2:18 passage. After God says, "It is not good for the man to be alone," He continues with, "I will make a helper suitable for him."

Now, before we dive in and explore this, a quick disclaimer. After the woman is created, God will preside over the first marriage in human history. Thus, this idea of a "helper suitable" is initiated in the context of a marriage relationship, and we'll first address it in this context. However, the principles guiding this idea of "helper suitable" transcend marriage relationships. So if you're reading this and you're not married, hang with me for a bit. For those of you who are married—well—buckle up.

God contends that Adam needs a "helper suitable" for him.[3]

When we hear the word "helper" in our twenty-first-century Western world, we generally think of it in terms of a subordinate role. As if the one who bears the title is functioning at a lesser level and must serve the one who is higher up. However, when it comes to the biblical notion of "helper," nothing could be farther from the truth.

The word translated as "helper" is the Hebrew word *ezer. Ezer* means "helper, aid, and/or strength."[4] It carries the idea of doing for another what they cannot do for themselves. *Ezer* is most often used in the Scriptures in connection with what God does for His people.[5] God is the ultimate *ezer*. Thus, *ezer* is not a word that means subordination or lesser than. It is a strong, edifying, praiseworthy word that connotes the indispensableness of the individual who bears the title. In the case of this Genesis passage, it's the woman!

What's interesting (and heartbreaking) is that this passage has been used throughout history to demean the essence of the woman in relationship to the man—as if she's lacking something. Yet the presence of *ezer* in connection to the woman doesn't indicate she's lacking. It indicates he's lacking. (And all the women say, "We've known that!") He needs her, and he needs her to be an *ezer* for him. But the need is reciprocal. Yes, he needs her, but she also needs him, and she needs him to be an *ezer* for her. They're both lacking and need each other to do what they cannot do for themselves.

This is not a passage establishing hierarchy but partnership. The husband and wife are co-owners of the marriage. She is not an employee. She is not a tagalong. She is not there for the purpose of executing his agenda, or to simply make sure his socks match. They are in this together, and they are to walk side by side into their collective future, doing what they can to help each other become better. As they assist each other in becoming better, they together become better. This was God's original design for marriage in the beginning, and it is still God's desire for marriage today.

Husbands, is this how you view your wives?

Wives, is this how you understand your husbands?

Couples, is this how you perceive the dynamics of your relationship?

Are you an *ezer*, or do you simply expect your spouse to be the primary *ezer*?

For many of us, there's enough in these last few paragraphs to keep us wrestling for some time. But there's more to the dynamics of this relationship. There's another word in the phrase "helper suitable."

As with "helper," the word translated as "suitable" doesn't accurately convey the nature of the Hebrew word. "Suitable" is the Hebrew word *kenegdo*. *Kenegdo* is a bit tricky to translate because it is a fusion of three words (which is typical of Hebrew). However, when understood holistically, and in its proper context, *kenegdo* means "one who stands in front of or opposite to."[6] It's the idea of someone who stands before you, facing you, opposing you, not simply allowing you to go whichever direction you choose. It's a word picture for how one is to relate to another. In more practical terms, we could say a *kenegdo* is someone who questions, confronts, challenges, and holds another accountable.

Now, I would imagine for most of us, we love the idea of an *ezer*. We love the idea of someone journeying alongside us, aiding us in our endeavors, and serving as an anchor of strength in our lives. Who wouldn't love and appreciate that? But let's be honest, we're not particularly fond of the *kenegdo* part, are we? We don't like the idea of being questioned, confronted, challenged, or held accountable for what we do.

We don't want to be questioned about our spending habits.

We don't want to be confronted about the impatience we're exhibiting with our kids.

We don't want to be challenged on why we're spending so much time at work.

We don't want to be held accountable for what we're viewing on the Internet.

We don't like this. "I'll take the *ezer*, but you can keep the *kenegdo*" would be our preference. And yet God declares that Adam needs an *ezer kenegdo*. Both facets are needed.

Some people are *ezer*s. They're amazing at coming alongside their partner and serving their needs, but they rarely challenge and question them. And some people are *kenegdo*s. They're not afraid to question, challenge, and confront, but at times it feels as though this is all they're interested in doing. They lack either the capacity or the willingness to be an encouraging source of strength. Quite frankly, they can be annoying and depressing to live with. They thrive on pushing back, but they're not helpful in moving the relationship forward.

But God's intention is not for us to be merely an *ezer* or a *kenegdo*. Our calling is to be an *ezer kenegdo*. Fused together, an *ezer kenegdo* is someone who questions, confronts, challenges, and holds another accountable, in love, for the purpose of aiding and strengthening the collective whole so together they move forward in a healthy and growing relationship, doing for each other what they're unable to do alone.

Struggle

Without the merging of both the *ezer* and the *kenegdo*, a relationship will not be everything God intends for it to be. But here's the catch. By virtue of the interaction of an *ezer kenegdo* relationship, a sense of conflict and struggle is not only implied, but understood.

For some reason, I missed this section in the relationship handbook. And I most certainly did not understand this going into my marriage. For as long as I can recall, I had been under the impression that struggles in a relationship were an indicator something was significantly wrong. As if couples were supposed to be so in step with each other that they instinctively knew what the other person needed at all times, always understood the other's feelings, and never allowed selfishness to creep in. And if there was any conflict or struggle, it was because there was something wrong with the relationship. Little did I realize this was a misconception. As the Genesis passage illuminates, when you say yes to relationships, you say yes to struggle. It's a given. It's part of the deal.

So the question isn't, *"Do you struggle?"* The question is, *"How do you struggle?"* And how you answer this question will affect every aspect of your relationships. There are basically two ways to struggle: you can either struggle *against* or you can struggle *with*.

Initially in our marriage, I struggled *against*. I wasn't willing to work through the struggles my wife and I were experiencing. So I struggled *against* my wife. I wouldn't answer her questions truthfully. I wouldn't let her in on things I was wrestling with. I would shut down. I would end the conversation. I would walk out of the room. I would allow her to cry for hours in our living room while I went to bed to escape the frustration.

I saw our struggles as obstacles to peace, and began to believe they were better left ignored than embraced. So I chose to live in denial. I didn't want to believe things were that bad. I didn't want to acknowledge we were failing miserably in our marriage. I wanted to believe I could push the problems aside and they would magically disappear over time. But that's never the case, and my approach left us in a stalemate.

Then something happened in our second year of marriage. Our church was having a marriage seminar, and my wife suggested we attend. My response was, "What for? We don't need that. What can we possibly learn from people who do seminars at a church?" Real optimistic, I know—especially from someone who now works in a church. But she was convinced we needed to go. After several failed attempts to get me to go, finally her persistence paid off. She signed us up for the seminar, which was slated to meet once a week for four weeks.

Like our first date, I wasn't expecting much. And like our first date, I was totally unprepared for what would happen. The marriage seminar changed the contour of our relationship. We learned marriages are complex relationships that need outside assistance from time to time, and every marriage could use some good counseling. We learned that struggles are not something to be ignored, but to be embraced and addressed. So we learned conflict resolution, and approaches to addressing our struggles at their cores. We learned nonviolent communication, and how to use our words in ways that were helpful in untangling the knots of struggle, rather than adding to them.[7]

What made the seminar so life-altering was that we learned how to struggle *with* each other, rather than *against*. And part of that struggling *with* meant we had to ask for help. We had to let others in on our struggles. We had to shatter the façade we'd created. Our marriage wasn't intact. We didn't have it all together. In fact, we didn't have much of anything together. We had to stop trying to make it on our own.

Did everything change overnight? No. But things began to change, especially for me. I could feel my calloused heart softening to my wife and to our marriage. Over the next several months our marriage was unrecognizable—at least to us. We were communicating better. We weren't fighting nearly as much. And when we did, it didn't last as long. We were actually beginning to experience a strange new phenomenon with each other. Joy. We were embracing our struggles, rather than denying them. And through it all, we were learning that struggle is normal, struggle is necessary, and struggle is the catalyst for building strength in a marriage.

It's like lifting weights. People do so to get stronger because they intuitively understand struggle builds muscle. Weights are a form of struggle. Nobody bench-presses air. There's nothing to it. There's no weight. There's no struggle. Without struggle, it's difficult to build muscle.

Any strong relationship will vouch that struggle builds muscle. Ask anyone who has a strong relationship what has contributed most to their strength, and I guarantee you they will tell you stories about the struggles they've worked through.

They will tell you stories about how he had an addiction.

Or she battled depression.

Or he lost a job.

Or she had cancer.

Or he got injured.

Or she mismanaged the finances.

Or he had an affair.

Or she tragically lost a loved one.

Or they had to work through issues of anger, pride, or selfishness.

Because it's in these moments a couple finds out what they're made of. It's in these moments they come to understand they can either struggle *against* or they can struggle *with*. Sometimes struggle comes because life happens, and it's no fault of our own. Sometimes struggle comes as a result of our own brokenness. Either way, struggle is part of life. It's how we deal with those struggles that makes all the difference. For those who choose to struggle *with*, their marriages become stronger in the long run. And that's exactly what my wife and I were learning to do.

Ezer Kenegdo Relationships

Our rekindled marriage opened up a whole new way of interacting together. We were now able to more fully live into our roles as *ezer kenegdo*s for one another. My wife had always been an *ezer* for me, but I had significantly limited her ability to be an *ezer kenegdo*. I hadn't been receptive to her help. I didn't allow myself to be questioned, confronted, challenged, or held accountable in love. By doing so, I had been denying my wife her God-given commandment and responsibility to be my *ezer kenegdo*.

Unfortunately, this happens in many marriages. I see it all the time. And it's not always with the husband. It happens with the wife as well. Husbands and wives, if you've created an ethos in your marriage where you run the show and your spouse is not allowed to question, confront, hold accountable, or challenge you in love, then you are denying them their God-given commandment and responsibility to be your *ezer kenegdo*. It's not healthy for you, and it's definitely not healthy for them.

God understands we need someone to challenge us, push us, and question us when we're doing things we probably shouldn't be doing. Without the challenge and accountability, we do what is right in our own eyes, and it can have devastating effects.

I was tired of seeing those effects in my own life and marriage. So I gave my wife permission to challenge, confront, and push me in ways I hadn't allowed before. And I am a different person because of it. I would not be where I am today (which is miles and miles beyond where I was when we first got married) without the grace of God, and the love, patience, and challenge my wife constantly gives. I am who I am because my wife makes me better. She does for me what I cannot do for myself. And she is someone who pushes me. She challenges me. She holds me accountable. And she does it all in love. I do not have the freedom to do whatever I want. And I am thankful for that. Because left to my own doing, I would go astray much farther and faster than what I am already prone to do.

We all need *ezer kenegdo* relationships. We need the challenge. We need the accountability. We need the struggle. It's what makes us stronger and healthier human beings. As Proverbs 27:17 wisely says, "As iron sharpens iron, so one person sharpens another."

Marriages naturally lend themselves to being these relationships, but we all need them, whether we're married or not. The principles of *ezer kenegdo* transcend marriage relationships, and have ramifications for all of life's important interactions. Our best friends can be *ezer kenegdo*s. Our teammates, on whatever team we find ourselves on, can be *ezer kenegdo*s. Our coworkers can even be *ezer kenegdo*s.

Furthermore, *ezer kenegdo* realities are possible and necessary even in tiered relationships, such as those that exist among teachers and students, coaches and players, employers and employees, and perhaps one of the most important relationships—parents and children. Let me offer an example of how *ezer kenegdo* principles can get fleshed out in such a relationship.

As parents, we ought to be *ezer kenegdo*s to our kids, and find a healthy balance between assisting them and challenging them. When my oldest was two years old, he took great pleasure in relocating every book from his bookshelf to the floor. I would come into his room and have no place to walk. Upon my arrival, he would begin to giggle. He knew I wouldn't allow his books to take up permanent residence on the floor, and my request to put them back would soon follow. After I'd make my request, he would look at me with his scintillating blue eyes and manufacture the most adorable of smiles, as if to say, "I am going to sucker you into cleaning up my mess."

Although amused, I wouldn't give in. I would tell him since he made the mess, he needed to clean up the mess. To which he'd reply, "Me can't do it. Daddy do it. Too hard." He'd have a good point. At times there were thirty or forty books spread out around his room. For a two-year-old, it probably felt like an insurmountable task.

In these moments, I had a few options. I could function as an *ezer* and clean up everything for him. I could function as a *kenegdo* and tell him he couldn't come out of his room until every last book was put away. Or I could live into being an *ezer kenegdo* by assisting and challenging him in the process. This last option seemed the most constructive.

So my response to my overwhelmed two-year-old was to tell him that Daddy would help him clean up his books, but he'd have to help as well. In a way, I was letting him know I was willing to struggle *with* him. And we'd begin picking up the books together. Now there were times when he'd refuse to do his part, and wouldn't contribute. He was struggling *against* me. So I'd leave the room. On my way out I'd inform him that when he was ready to do his part, I'd return and help him finish the task. Inevitably, after weighing his options for a couple of minutes, he'd request my assistance, and together we'd return his books to their rightful place.

It was my attempt at being an *ezer kenegdo* to my boy. Whether your kids are two, or seven, or seventeen, I would urge you to think about how you can be an *ezer kenegdo* to them. How can you assist and strengthen them, and in the process challenge and confront them in a helpful way?

Going this route will be more difficult, because it will involve struggle. It's easier to just do their science project than to sit down and struggle through it with them. It's easier to tell them to figure out their math problems alone rather than taking time to explain to them what they don't understand. It's easier to do everything for them or nothing for them, because these options avoid struggle. But an *ezer kenegdo* parent embraces the struggle, and strives for balance between assisting and challenging.

And that's the balance we seek in all the important relationships we find ourselves in.

Think about who the *ezer kenegdo*s are in your life.

Who do you struggle with who makes you better?

Who have you given permission to challenge you?

Who holds you accountable?

Who really knows what's going on in your life?

And then ask yourself who you are an *ezer kenegdo* to.

Who are you pushing to become better?

Who do you have clearance to question and confront?

Who do you serve as a source of strength for?

Who are you helping become better than what they can be on their own?

Sadly, Samson didn't have this kind of relationship. He lived his life in such a way that he did what he wanted, when he wanted, and however he wanted to do it. And I believe it was a significant detriment to his life. The writer of Ecclesiastes concludes, "Two are better than one, because they have a good return for their labor: if either of them falls down, one can help the other up. But pity anyone who falls and has no one to help them up" (4:9–10). I believe Samson ran amuck, in part, because he was a lone ranger. He journeyed with no one. He had no friends. He had no accountability. He had no one to help him up when he fell. He had no one to push him, challenge him, confront him, or engage him in the kind of struggle that would have strengthened his life. He did not have an *ezer kenegdo*.

Without people who love us enough to challenge us, to push us, to confront us, to help us get back on track when we derail, we simply don't become everything God desires for us to become. We weren't designed to journey alone. We were designed to journey with others in an *ezer kenegdo* relationship. We were designed for struggle.

CHAPTER 6

Gotta Have Blue Eyes

I joined the golf team my senior year of high school because I needed more balance. Growing up, my great love was basketball. The joke during my high school years was the only girl I'd date had to be round, orange, and bounce really well. I did date a wonderful girl my senior year, which unintentionally curbed the stigma, but the joke rang true for much of my high school days.

The trouble I was having with basketball was burnout. By the end of my sophomore and junior years, I was running on fumes—more mentally than physically. So when my senior year came around, I joined the golf team in the fall, tempered my intense preseason basketball workouts, and entered into a rhythm that brought not only balance to my life, but also great joy. Along with basketball, I grew up playing golf, and enjoyed it very much. It ended up being a welcome change not only for my rhythm but for my hair as well.

I found out quickly that the golfers on my team, and those from the surrounding schools, were sporting a look quite different from my own. Since I was seeking more balance in my life, I decided to contrast my normal short hair basketball look with the longer, more unrestrained look that appeared to be the golfer norm. I particularly enjoyed having my curls wrap around the sides of my Titleist hat.

The look would have to go when basketball season came around, but for the time being, it worked.

It was a fad, a style, a way of fitting in.

It wasn't encouraged.

It wasn't essential.

It wasn't required.

But for Samson it was.

Not to play golf, of course, but for adherence to the Nazirite vow. The stipulation recorded in Numbers 6 states, "During the entire period of their Nazirite vow, no razor may be used on their head. They must be holy until the period of their dedication to the LORD is over; they must let their hair grow long" (v. 5).

Samson's hair would have been a lot longer than mine—both on his face and on his head. A Nazirite man wasn't allowed to cut either. I wasn't allowed to have facial hair (couldn't grow it anyway), and even though I could grow out the top, my sides couldn't drop past my ears owing to my school's "antishabbiness" regulations. I got away with my hair being a couple of inches longer than my teammates' because of the coiled effect my curls would perform when gelled, but Samson's overall appearance would have been significantly different from mine.

I fit in. He would've stuck out. And that seems to be part of the point.

But there seems to be more to it. If God's only purpose in requiring long hair was to make the Nazirite stand out, He could've required something else. He could've required a Nazirite to wear a certain kind of tunic, or a flashy belt. He could've required an earring or some other defining piece of jewelry. God could've required the men to sport a beardless face to accentuate a mandated Fu Manchu. That would've definitely garnered some attention! And yet God required long hair.

The reason seems to lie in what the hair symbolized.

To understand the symbolism, you need to know something significant about the Hebrew language. Contrary to Greek and English, which are noun-based languages, Hebrew is a verb-based language. Meaning, verbs sit at the core of the language, and all subsequent parts of speech (nouns, adjectives, etc.) are derived from verbs. So when dealing with a noun, it's particularly helpful to understand the verb it was derived from as it can provide additional meaning behind the noun.

The Hebrew word for "Nazirite" is *nazir*. *Nazir* is derived from the Hebrew verb *nazar*, which means, "to dedicate, consecrate, or separate."[1]

A Nazirite was someone who committed themselves entirely to the service of God. They were sold out to the things of God, and all attention and devotion were directed to God and living in obedience to His will. Therefore, a Nazirite was to be a visible example of what it looked like to live completely in tune with God.

The Nazirite's intensified allegiance and service to God for the length of the vow placed them in a unique relationship with God, thus separating themselves from others. Additionally, the Nazirite separated themselves by abstaining from certain acts (cutting one's hair, consuming anything from the grapevine, being in the vicinity of something dead) permitted to the common person.

Of the three restrictions, only the long hair was the constant, visible indicator one had taken on the Nazirite vow. Thus, the long hair served as the Nazirite's visible symbol of their dedication to God.[2]

But there's more. To understand the rest of it, there's something else you need to know about the Hebrew language. Words derived from the same verb are linked in meaning to each other.

Like *nazir* ("Nazirite"), another word derived from the verb *nazar* ("to dedicate, consecrate, or separate") is *nezer*, which means "crown."[3]

Now you may be wondering, "What possible connection is there between a crown and being a Nazirite?"

A crown is something worn by an individual in a unique position. It sits on top of one's head, and symbolizes the authority to rule.

The long hair was the Nazirite's "crown." It symbolized the unique relationship between the Nazirite and God. However, what the "crown" did not symbolize was the Nazirite's authority to rule. As we've explored, to take on the Nazirite vow was to wholly submit to the purposes of God. Thus, the "crown" did not symbolize the Nazirite's rule, but God's rule.

A Nazirite was called to live *under* the rule and reign of God. Since a crown or one's hair sits on *top* of one's head, it reminded the Nazirite they weren't above themselves. God was above them. They weren't their own authority, and they couldn't simply do what they wanted. And the visual, physical reminder of this reality was the Nazirite's hair, the "crown" of God. This is why a Nazirite was required to shave their head if they broke one of the restrictions of the vow, because it indicated that, at a particular moment, they didn't live under the rule and reign of God.[4]

By the way, this is one of the reasons why many Jews wear yarmulkes (or *kippah*s) today. It's a visual, physical reminder that something is above them. They are not their own standard. God is above them, and they are to live under the rule and reign of God—represented by the yarmulke.

So the long hair was the Nazirite's "crown," the visible symbol of their dedication to God reminding them they were not their own authority, but they were to live under the rule of God. It served as a daily reminder for the Nazirite to live fully into the vow they took, and to further remind them of their calling to be a public example of what it looks like to live according to God's rules and desires.

If you'll recall from the introduction, a Nazirite vow was voluntary. However, for Samson it was not. He did not choose it. It was chosen for him. Which can be problematic. Because even though the directive came from Samson's Creator, who has every right to require such a lifestyle, there's something about us humans that we chafe against not having a say in a matter. We don't like being told what to do, even if it's the best thing for us. We struggle with this. And so did Samson.

The Effects of Seeing

As the curtain is drawn on the adult life of Samson, this struggle between living according to God's desires or his own sits center stage. Notice what happens first. "Samson went down to Timnah, and at Timnah he *saw* one of the daughters of the Philistines" (Judg. 14:1, ESV, emphasis mine).

And then notice Samson's first recorded words, coming immediately after visiting Timnah. "Then he came up and told his father and mother, 'I *saw* one of the daughters of the Philistines at Timnah. Now get her for me as my wife'" (Judg. 14:2, ESV, emphasis mine).

Note that Samson's first actions and words are about how he "saw" a Philistine woman. This may seem trivial at best, but the implications are far reaching, not the least of which that it leads to his demanding that his parents get her as his wife.

Over and over again, God explicitly states that the Children of Israel are not to marry foreign women. This prohibition is first recorded in Exodus 34 when the Children of Israel are at Mount Sinai receiving instructions from God on how to live. God, in speaking to Moses about the current inhabitants of the land of Canaan, states:

> "Be careful not to make a treaty with those who live in the land; for when they prostitute themselves to their gods and sacrifice to

them, they will invite you and you will eat their sacrifices. And when you choose some of their daughters as wives for your sons and those daughters prostitute themselves to their gods, they will lead your sons to do the same." (vv. 15–16)

In Deuteronomy 7, as the Israelites are east of the Jordan River on the plains of Moab (just opposite Jericho), and preparing to enter the land of Canaan, Moses reminds them with these words:

"When the LORD your God brings you into the land you are entering to possess and drives out before you many nations—the Hittites, Girgashites, Amorites, Canaanites, Perizzites, Hivites and Jebusites, seven nations larger and stronger than you—and when the LORD your God has delivered them over to you and you have defeated them, then you must destroy them totally. Make no treaty with them, and show them no mercy. Do not intermarry with them. Do not give your daughters to their sons or take their daughters for your sons, for they will turn your children away from following me to serve other gods, and the LORD's anger will burn against you and will quickly destroy you." (vv. 1–4)

And in the event any of the Israelites didn't remember this after entering Canaan and subduing many of its inhabitants, Joshua reminds them, saying:

"But if you turn away and ally yourselves with the survivors of these nations that remain among you and if you intermarry with them and associate with them, then you may be sure that the LORD your God will no longer drive out these nations before you. Instead, they will become snares and traps for you, whips on your backs and thorns in your eyes, until you perish from this good land, which the LORD your God has given you." (Joshua 23:12–13)

At Sinai.

On the plains of Moab.

In the land of Canaan.

The instructions are the same: *Do not* intermarry with the foreigners in the land.

This is because God knows the fastest track to derailment for the Children of Israel is intermarriage. Please understand, God's issue isn't that they're foreigners or that they have a different ethnic background. God's concern is about Israel living in the land of Canaan, a place where the social and theological systems will inevitably lure the Israelites away from following God. Especially when that social, theological system involves highly sexual pagan worship.[5] The last thing God wants is for His people to get derailed by this.

Therefore, when Samson demands to have this Philistine woman as his wife, it's wrong on at least three levels.

First, it clearly violates the commandment of God.

Second, it puts Samson's parents in a conundrum because, according to Deuteronomy 7, they aren't allowed to obtain a foreign woman for their son—which is exactly what Samson demands of them.

Third, Samson violates a social custom, which in many ways for the ancient people was as severe as breaking one of God's commandments. This social custom was that of arranged marriages. We implicitly see this in the prohibition of Deuteronomy 7 that the parents not obtain a foreigner for their child, as arranged marriages were the norm of the day. This is why Samson includes his parents in his desire, which wasn't uncommon. Children often had some say in the process.

However, the violation comes in Samson's demanding that his parents do what he wants. This would've been offensive not only to Samson's parents, but also to the community at large. It's a communal culture, rooted in honor and shame, where the decisions you make affect not only your family, but also your community.[6]

What's more, it's a Philistine woman. The Philistines have been oppressively ruling the Israelites for forty years (see Judg. 13:1). Samson is raised up for the purpose of addressing this oppression, and yet he wants to marry into it.

Samson's parents, who clearly do not wish to disobey God, or break the social customs of the day, are deeply troubled by this. It's no wonder they respond with, "Isn't there an acceptable woman among your relatives or among all our people? Must you go to the uncircumcised Philistines to get a wife?" (Judg. 14:3).[7]

In reply to his parents' earnest and desperate plea, Samson irreverently petitions, "Get her for me, for she is right in my *eyes*" (Judg. 14:3, ESV, emphasis mine).

This is where the story gets fascinating. A theme has been introduced into the narrative, and it's at this moment we begin to pick up on what's going on.

We previously observed that Samson's first actions and words were about how he "saw" a Philistine woman in Timnah. And now he states, "she is right in my own eyes."

There's something going on with Samson's "eyes." The narrator is being very intentional in how they're recording this storyline. Three times in three verses, there's a reference to the eyes. And in case we haven't picked up on the theme, the narrator attests only four verses later, "Then he [Samson] went down and talked with the woman, and she was right in Samson's *eyes*" (Judg. 14:7, ESV, emphasis mine).

The eyes are the filters through which we make decisions on how we're going to live. Our eyes set our direction. And depending upon the course our eyes set, they'll determine not only the path we walk, but how we walk it.

According to the story, Samson is doing what is right in his own eyes.

It's not right in God's eyes.

It's not right in his parents' eyes.

It's not right in his community's eyes.

But it's right in Samson's eyes.

And for Samson, his eyes are the only ones that matter.

When Eyes Lead Us Astray

I remember golfing with my friend Corbett one afternoon after several days of rain. The course was wet, and the large areas of standing water were roped off to prevent golf carts from tearing up the vulnerable grass. My second shot on the seventh hole landed in a roped-off area that appeared to be the size of Texas. Hiking shoes seemed more appropriate for the walk to my ball than golf shoes. What's more, we didn't see any standing water. Annoyed from circumnavigating countless ropes the first six holes, and feeling justified in our reasoning, we decided it was time to disregard the rules.

Corbett drove us up to the roped area, placing the front bumper against the rope. Leaning over the front of the cart from the passenger side, I reached out and lifted up the rope. While I held the rope high above our heads, Corbett slowly drove our roofless cart under it. Once through, I let the rope go, failing to realize it had not cleared our golf clubs—specifically, my five-iron. We made it three feet before our cart was yanked to a halt. Wondering what in the world just happened, I quickly spun around in time to see my five-iron give way to the tension of the rope, causing the dark green metal stake responsible for supporting the rope to slingshot forward. The corner of the stake struck me a half inch from my eye. The small scar reminds me to this day that doing what was right in my own eyes nearly cost me an eye.

Samson wasn't so fortunate.

Coming on the heels of Samson's spending an evening with a prostitute he "saw" in Gaza (see Judg. 16:1), his reckless behavior of doing what is right in his own eyes finally catches up with him when Delilah gets the better of him. And then what do the Philistines do after cutting Samson's hair? They tear out his eyes. As the narrator recounts, "Then the Philistines seized him, gouged out his eyes and took him down to Gaza" (Judg. 16:21).

Granted, one could argue this was a strategic move on the part of the Philistines to permanently subdue their nemesis, and it was. But as we've observed, there's more going on under the sea. Samson's eyes played a leading role in getting him to where he is, and when he loses them, he loses more than just his eyesight.

Which makes his prayer in the temple of Dagon all the more interesting and understandable. You'll recall that prior to the culminating moment of Samson's revenge, he prays, "Sovereign LORD, remember me. Please, God, strengthen me just once more, and let me with one blow get revenge on the Philistines for my two eyes" (Judg. 16:28).

Notably, owing to the Hebrew construction, it's slightly more accurate to translate this last phrase "for one of my two eyes."[8] Samson's been disgraced with the loss of his eyes, and he's seeking to regain his honor. According to his reasoning, the death of three thousand Philistines only justifies the loss of one of his eyes! (I wonder what would've justified the loss of both?) In his eyes, or lack thereof, he's that important and that valuable. The pride is still present, and everything is still about him.

The Samson narrative begins with Samson speaking of "seeing" a Philistine woman and then demanding to have her as his wife, all because she is "right in his own eyes." It continues with him "seeing" a prostitute in Gaza. And it culminates with him killing three thousand men and women, including himself, because he's furious he lost his eyes, and wants to avenge the loss of one of them.

But it doesn't end here.

The Samson narrative concludes with "He had led Israel twenty years" (Judg. 16:31).

At first read, this sounds impressive.

Twenty years of ruling sounds like a long time.

What's more, such a statement seems to imply that Samson was a successful judge and ruler—that he accomplished what he was commissioned to do (even though we'd all likely agree that his means of doing so were reckless and destructive).

Let's see what we can uncover.

If you read or survey the book of Judges, you will find a total of twelve judges. By the way, "judge" here isn't referring to someone behind a big wooden desk with a gavel in hand. It refers to someone who serves as a leader among the people, guiding and delivering them in their time of need. So there are twelve judges—twelve men and women are given their shot at leading the Israelites.[9] Some get a lot of airtime in the book of Judges. Some get very little. Some rule for an extended period of time. Some for a short period of time, relatively speaking. Based on their length of rule and the airtime they receive in Judges, these twelve individuals have been traditionally subdivided into two groups—Major Judges (Othniel, Ehud, Deborah, Gideon, Jephthah, and Samson) and Minor Judges (Shamgar, Tola, Jair, Ibzan, Elon, and Abdon).

Notice in the chart below the key information depicted in the

Judge	Reference	Tribe	Oppressor	Period of Oppression	Period of Rest
Othniel	3:7–11	Judah	Mesopotamians	8 years	40 years
Ehud	3:12–30	Benjamin	Moabites	18 years	80 years
Shamgar	3:31		Philistines		
Deborah	Chs 4–5	Ephraim	Canaanites	20 years	40 years
Gideon	Chs 6–8	Manasseh	Midianites	7 years	40 years
Tola	10:1–2	Issachar			23 years
Jair	10:3–5	Manasseh (Gilead)			22 years
Jephthah	10:6–12:7	Manasseh (Gilead)	Ammonites	18 years	6 years
Ibzan	12:8–10	Asher (or Zebulun)			7 years
Elon	12:11–12	Zebulun			10 years
Abdon	12:13–15	Ephraim			8 years
Samson	Chs 13–16	Dan	Philistines	40 years	20 years

book of Judges about these judges. Naturally, we are given more information on the Major Judges than the Minor Judges.

Allow me to point out a few observations with respect to Samson.

Samson is one of only two judges whose "period of rest" (i.e., length of rule) is *less than* the "period of oppression" preceding his rule. (The "period of oppression" is the length of time the Israelites were under the oppressive control of a foreign power.)

Samson's narrative gets the most airtime of any of the judges, and yet six judges have *longer* "periods of rest" than his—two of which are Minor Judges.

Samson's "period of rest" is *only* twenty years in length. Excluding Jephthah, whose story was tragic like Samson's, notice the "period of rest" among the other Major Judges:

Othniel—40 years
Ehud—80 years
Deborah—40 years
Gideon—40 years

The pattern of "40 years" is obvious. The number 40 is significant in the biblical text. It connotes a period of testing, trial, and/or accomplishment. To rule for forty years was a mark of strength, endurance, and achievement. Ehud was fortunate enough to experience two sets of forty-year periods of rest. King David, the most celebrated king in the Old Testament, will rule for forty years following the time of the Judges.[10] But Samson rules for only twenty years—half the length of the desired time. And in comparison to the other judges, Samson's rule isn't impressive. In fact, it's disappointing.

What's more, the last verse of Judges 15 reads, "Samson led Israel for twenty years in the days of the Philistines" (v. 20).

Sound familiar? That's how Judges 16 ends, which we noted above. Again, this may seem trivial at first, but this is the beauty of the biblical text. Nothing is random, and when you begin to pick up on how these ancient writers recorded these stories, you see how they tip you off to other facets of the text.

With no other judge is the length of rule given in the middle of the narrative. In each case, when the length of rule is given, it appears at the end of the judge's story—never during. And yet with Samson, it appears not only at the end of his story, but also in the middle of it, which seems to signify Samson "retired." His length of rule did not end with his death, as it did for the other judges. His length of rule ended of his own accord. Not only did Samson struggle with his responsibility to address the oppression of the Philistines, but he believed he could opt out of his calling to God at any time. And he did.

So when we're told that Samson ruled for twenty years, I would submit to you this isn't a statement of accomplishment. It's an indictment. It's a statement of disappointment. Samson lived by the motto of doing what was right in his own eyes, and this is what it led to. And sadly, it had monumental impact not only on his life, but on the lives of others as well.

Right in Their Own Eyes

Again, there are twelve judges in the book of Judges. Samson is the twelfth and final judge. Now we would expect in a book called "Judges" that when the final judge died, the book would end. However, this isn't the case. Following Samson's temple collapse act, five chapters of stories ensue.

And they're all telling.

Let's jump into Judges 18 for a few moments. Notice how this chapter begins:

In those days Israel had no king. And in those days the tribe of the Danites was seeking a place of their own where they might settle, because they had not yet come into an inheritance among the tribes of Israel. (v. 1)

The Danites are one of the twelve tribes of Israel. But they're not just any tribe. They're the tribe Samson belonged to. Samson was a Danite.[11] So this story is about Samson's people.

The problem is they don't have a place to live. Which tells us they were unable to secure their tribal inheritance—the land allotted to them upon entering the land of Canaan. This is highly problematic. Every tribe was given an allotment of land, and it was their responsibility to secure it from the nations residing there. According to Judges 1:34, "The Amorites confined the Danites to the hill country, not allowing them to come down into the plain." So the tribe of Dan gets squeezed up into the hill country, and after struggling with their inability to claim their allotted land (both during and after Samson's rule), they concede and essentially declare, "We're done with this."

They then commission five of their leading men to scout the land looking for a new place to live. They make their way to the north-

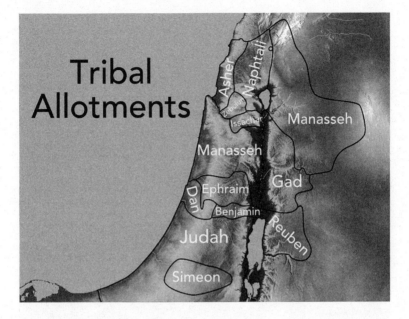

Tribal Allotments

ernmost part of the country and come upon a city called Laish. As recorded in the text, they "*saw* that the people were living in safety, like the Sidonians, at peace and secure. And since their land lacked nothing, they were prosperous. Also, they lived a long way from the Sidonians and had no relationship with anyone else" (Judg. 18:7, emphasis mine).

In their eyes (pun intended), they "saw" this city as a prime candidate for their tribe's relocation. Subsequently, they return to their people, report their findings, and make the recommendation to attack Laish. The people accept the recommendation. And as the narrator recounts it, "Then they took what Micah had made,[12] and his priest, and went on to Laish, against a people at peace and secure. They attacked them with the sword and burned down their city. There was no one to rescue them because they lived a long way from Sidon and had no relationship with anyone else. The city was

in a valley near Beth Rehob. The Danites rebuilt the city and settled there. They named it Dan after their ancestor Dan, who was
born to Israel—though the city used to be called Laish" (Judg.
18:27–29).

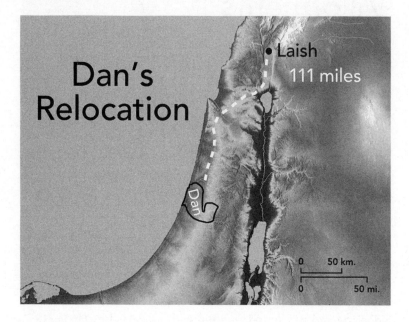

There the Danites set up for themselves the idol, and Jonathan son
of Gershom, the son of Moses, and his sons were priests for the tribe
of Dan until the time of the captivity of the land. They continued to
use the idol Micah had made, all the time the house of God was in
Shiloh. (Judges 18:30–31)

The generation following Samson has no place to live.

They concede and abandon their ancestral land—their inheritance from God.

They trek 111 miles away.

They attack a peaceful and unsuspecting people.

They set up for themselves an idol (even though the tabernacle was at Shiloh[13]).

And they worship the idol for over three hundred and fifty years,[14] until they are destroyed.[15]

At this point, the evidence for Samson being a successful leader isn't looking so good.

But let's press this a little further.

Arguably some of the ugliest, bloodiest, most depraved chapters of the entire Bible are the last five chapters of the book of Judges. Following the story of Micah and his idol, and the Danites' relocation, we encounter a story encompassing attempted gang rape as well as the murder of a woman who was gang raped to death over a period of several hours. Following this unspeakable horror, the husband of the murdered woman cuts her ravaged body into twelve pieces and sends them throughout the land. Subsequently a civil war breaks out, and thirty-five thousand Israelites are ruthlessly slaughtered at the hands of their own brothers. The massacre leaves the tribe of Benjamin nearly wiped out. To remedy the situation, young Israelite girls are kidnapped from other towns to repopulate the Benjamin tribe.

Ugly.

Broken.

Disturbing.

Perplexing.

It makes you wonder what would motivate these people to engage in such grotesque and destructive kinds of behavior. The answer, according to the text, is found in this statement: "In those days Israel had no king; everyone did what was right in his own eyes."

This is how these final chapters of Judges begin and end. This is the declaration that bookends these appalling stories. This is the summary statement that first shows up six verses into Judges 17 and appears as the last sentence in the book of Judges. Furthermore, the abbreviated version—"In those days Israel had no king"—makes an appearance multiple times within these bookends.[16]

Here's what's fascinating. Prior to the Samson narrative, there isn't a single reference to anyone in the book of Judges doing what was right in their own eyes. Not one! And yet the moment we encounter the grown Samson, we're introduced to a man who "sees" a Philistine woman, desires to marry her, even though such action would be in direct disobedience to God, demands that his parents violate the commands of God and the customs of the community by obtaining her to be his wife, and offends his parents and the community in the process all because she was right in his own eyes. And the remainder of his story is Samson living more fully into doing what was right in his own eyes, until he loses his eyes and goes to his death seeking revenge for the loss of one of his eyes. Furthermore, a host of people follow Samson's leading, doing what is right in their own eyes, and it leads to the most horrific chapters in the Bible.

This is what the author wants us to "see."

Samson set a precedent. He set an example others followed. He took his eyes off what was right, chose to do what was right in his own eyes, and subsequently did not do what was right in God's eyes. Proverbs 12:15 states, "The way of a fool is right in his own eyes, but a wise man is he who listens to counsel" (NASB).

The effects of Samson's choices were devastating, not only to his life, but to the lives of those around him,[17] and to those who followed after him. Samson led an entire generation astray because of the choices he made. And I'm willing to bet he didn't have a clue as to the effects his decisions would have on others. But then neither do we. It's easy to get caught up in the notion that our choices don't affect others. We fall prey to believing we can do what we want and it won't impact others. But it does.

If you're struggling with unforgiveness or pornography or an eating disorder, it's affecting others. You may think it's your own thing on the side, and that it doesn't affect others because they're unaware of it, but you're fooling yourself. Even if they don't know what's going on, it's affecting them, because it's affecting you. We're not isolated individuals who can limit our effect upon others. We're integrated beings whose lives bleed onto one another, and we impact one another positively or negatively.

This is why it's so important we have a standard to follow and accountability to hold us in check. It's why we must also be careful about what we allow to influence our lives, because we'll inevitably pass it on. And others will inevitably pick it up.

As a father of three small children, I've seen firsthand how this plays out in my house. It began with my oldest as I was shaving in the bathroom one morning. He came in, and with his less-than-two-year-old eyes, he stared up at me in amazement. Later on that day, I saw him sitting in the corner of our living room, holding a toy spoon, making shaving strokes across his face.

I've seen it in how my kids relate to one another. My daughter is two years younger than my eldest son. Like many second-born children, she did everything earlier than he did. She learned to feed herself earlier, walk earlier, and talk earlier. Why? She saw what her brother did, and she wanted to do it as well. She emulated what she saw. She still does.

What's true of my kids is true of us all. We emulate what we see.

Your kids are watching you.

Your siblings are watching you.

Your friends are watching you.

Your coworkers are watching you.

People you don't even know are watching you.

What we do matters. How we choose to live our lives matters. The example we set matters. They matter not only to our well-being, but to the well-being of others. We may not have the same clout as Samson, but we will affect those around us and, to one varying degree or another, those who come after us. We must deal with the junk in our lives so it won't affect others, because we will pass on our traits to our kids and to those who seek to emulate our lives. Therefore, we have to get things right.

There's a lot at stake. Not only for us, and for those we impact, but *also* for God. Which leads us to the other facet of this discussion.

Tassels on Garments

There's an obscure passage in Numbers 15 I doubt many Christians have read, or would at least remember reading. It's one of those passages you can read and not think much of. However, to a religious Jew, it's a passage they not only know well, but will recite more than twenty thousand times in the course of their lifetime.

It's one of the three biblical passages that comprise the "Shema,"[18] recited every morning and evening by religious Jews. This recitation has been going on for thousands of years, and without question would've been part of Jesus' daily rhythms as well. This was one of the central passages he oriented his life around.

Here's the passage found in Numbers 15:37–41:

The LORD said to Moses, "Speak to the Israelites and say to them: 'Throughout the generations to come you are to make tassels on the corners of your garments, with a blue cord on each tassel. You will have these tassels to look at and so you will remember all the commands of the LORD, that you may obey them and not prostitute yourselves by chasing after the lusts of your own hearts and eyes. Then you will remember to obey all my commands and will be consecrated to your God. I am the LORD your God, who brought you out of Egypt to be your God. I am the LORD your God.'"

The anchoring commandment is for the Israelites to tie tassels on the corners of their outer garments. The tassels represented God's instructions or commandments. God's desire was to provide His people with a visual, tactile reminder—something they would see and touch every day—that would remind them they were in relationship with Him and they were to honor their commitment to God by following His ways.

Although tying tassels on garments seems a bit odd to us in a twenty-first-century context, the purpose we understand well. When my wife and I stood in front of family and friends and exchanged vows, we also exchanged rings. The wedding rings served as a physical symbol of our marriage relationship and the vows we had just made to each other. And from that point forward, whenever we see our rings, we are reminded to forsake all others and maintain our focus on the one we've committed our lives to. The tassels served a similar function.

What interests me most about this passage, however, is the seemingly minor detail God includes about having a "blue cord on each tassel."

The Hebrew word for "blue" is *tekhelet*. It shows up forty-nine times in the Hebrew Scriptures—thirty-four times in the book of Exodus alone. The reason for the lopsided appearance is due almost entirely to the construction of the tabernacle. Blue, along with purple and scarlet, were the principle colors used in the tabernacle design. Thus, the color blue played a leading role in the visual representation of God's dwelling here on earth.

When it came to the priestly garments, however, the color blue played *the* leading role. In Exodus 28, the artisans are instructed by God to "make the robe of the ephod all of blue [*tekhelet*]" (v. 31, NASB). Blue was the color of the priests.

Although this is helpful, by itself it doesn't explain why God would require all of the Israelites to wear a blue tassel. But coupled together with what ensues in Exodus 19, after the Israelites arrive at Mount Sinai, the answer begins to emerge.

Leading up to this point, God has rescued and redeemed the Israelites from the life-sucking slavery in Egypt with the Ten Plagues. The Israelites have crossed the Red Sea[19] on dry ground, while the mighty Egyptian army drowned under collapsing walls of water. The Israelites have navigated the precarious circumstances of the Sinai Desert for six weeks, and have finally arrived at Mount Sinai, the destination stipulated to Moses at the burning bush.[20] Moses now ascends the mountain, and God speaks these words to him to relay to the Israelites:

"You yourselves have seen what I did to Egypt, and how I carried you on eagles' wings and brought you to myself. Now if you obey me fully and keep my covenant, then out of all nations you will be my treasured possession. Although the whole earth is mine, you will be for me a kingdom of priests and a holy nation." (Exodus 19:4–6)

Treasured possession.
Kingdom of priests.
Holy nation.

These are phrases of identity and calling, each encapsulating a host of meanings and implications. But the one most relevant to our conversation is that of Israel being a "kingdom of priests." To comprehend and appreciate the significance of such a designation, we must understand the role of a priest in the ancient world and the historical setting Israel emerges from.

For over four hundred years, the Children of Israel resided in the land of Egypt. Egypt is arguably the most theocratic society the world has ever seen. Over fifteen hundred gods and goddesses have been identified in connection with Egyptian worship. With gods and goddesses come temples and priesthoods, something the Israelites understood well after having been engrossed in this culture for such a long time. They knew how the religious system worked.

When you went to offer your worship to a god at his temple, you wouldn't meet with the god. The god was off limits. So what did you do? You met with one of the priests. Why? Because the priest mediated to the people on the god's behalf. They stood in the gap between the god and the worshipper. And they did so as the god's chosen ambassador, authorized to act on the god's behalf, and therefore functioned as the physical hands and feet of the god. Priests were seen as the best human representation of what the god was like. So when you met with a priest, it was as if you were meeting with the god himself. This was the essence of what it meant to be a priest in the ancient world.[21]

Perhaps you've heard the phrase "the medium is the message." Marshall McLuhan coined it in 1964, in a groundbreaking book on media theory.[22] McLuhan believed that "the form of a message (print, visual, musical, etc.) determines the ways in which that message will be perceived."[23] This means the medium (which carries the message) creates a symbiotic relationship with the message, and therefore influences how the recipient encounters the message.

A "priest" was an ancient embodiment of McLuhan's idea that "the medium is the message." The priest was the medium through which the message of the god was communicated to the world, and it was in the behavior of the priest that the message of the god was encountered by others. Being a priest in the ancient world was a calling that carried with it colossal implications.

And the living God of the universe says to the Israelites at Sinai, "I want you to be that for me. I want you to be my priests. I want you to stand in the gap between me and the rest of the world. I want you to serve as my hands and feet in the world, as my authorized ambassadors. I want you to live your lives in such a way that when the world interacts with you, it's as if they are interacting with me!" In short, "I want you to be my message!"

What a staggering declaration.

At this moment, Israel receives her fundamental identity and calling as the people of God. As a kingdom of priests, they are to be the medium through which the world encounters the message of God. Their very lives will communicate to the world what God is like. They are to put God on display by what they say; how they live; how they treat their families, their friends, strangers they encounter—no matter who it is, they are to be like God to them. Everything they do is to point the way for others to see what God is like.

Furthermore, Israel understands they have been rescued and redeemed from slavery for a purpose. God has work for them to do. At the core of being a priest is service. Priests are not chosen for privilege, but for service. Israel's salvation and redemption were never the end game. They were only the beginning. The purpose of their salvation and redemption was to bring them into a relationship with God. And in doing so, God was able to give them a new identity, and commission them for service in His redemptive, worldwide agenda. God wanted His message to reach the world, and He desired that message to be brought through the medium of His people. As priests of the living God, they were to be the message.[24]

And God obviously wants to be represented and presented well. So it makes sense that immediately after declaring His people a "kingdom of priests," God begins giving the commandments. The commandments articulate how Israel is to relate to God and to one another in order to become the message God wants communicated to the world. They are going to be a "kingdom of priests," and therefore they must live into the message God wants the world to encounter.

This is what it means to be a follower of God. This is the calling of those who consider themselves God's people. As far as God is concerned, when you say yes to God, you say yes to priesthood. God called them priests back then. He called them priests again in the New Testament. Peter, writing to followers of Jesus scattered throughout ancient Asia Minor (modern-day Turkey) proclaims, "But you are a chosen people, a royal priesthood, a holy nation, God's special possession, that you may declare the praises of him who called you out of darkness into his wonderful light" (1 Pet. 2:9).

And as a daily, visual reminder of this profound reality, God says, "Tie tassels on the corners of your garments, and make sure one strand of each tassel is blue." As the tassels would flop around throughout the course of the day, the people would be reminded of their instructions from God on how to live. And as their eyes caught the scintillating blue against the white, they would be reminded they bore the priestly color because they served as priests on behalf of the living God of the universe. Blue is the color of God's people.

Now, if you're reading this and you're a Christian, there are some serious implications to this reality. So allow me to take the remaining few pages of this chapter and speak directly to you about the implications.

To wear the color blue is to be reminded, "You are the message."

The medium is the message, and we are the medium, and therefore the message. Which means, you and I are always communicating a message about God. If people in your class, or at work, or on your team know you're a Christian, then they're viewing a message. We don't have the luxury of choosing whether we want to be communicating a message or not. If we're breathing... too late!

We must recognize we're communicating a message about God all the time and in all facets of life. We do so in our interactions with those we love most. We do so in our treatment of coworkers and customers, or in how we do our work. We communicate a message in the jokes we tell, in the way we dress, and in the language we use. We say something about God in how we conduct ourselves on the sports field, in our city league games, in how we use our money, or in our interaction (or lack thereof) with the poor and needy.

As followers of God, we bear the name of God. It's like we walk around wearing a blue sports jersey with God's name written on our upper back.[25] Everything we do speaks to the name we bear. And we are called to carry the name of God well. In fact, this gets at the essence of one of the Ten Commandments. In Exodus 20, God states, "You shall not take the name of the LORD your God in vain, for the LORD will not hold him guiltless who takes his name in vain" (v. 7, ESV). Typically, this commandment has been interpreted in our modern context to discourage the use of God's name as a swear word. Although true, this is a limited understanding of its intended purpose.

The word translated as "take" is the Hebrew verb *nasa*, a word we discussed earlier which means to "lift up, take, carry, or bear." The word translated as "vain" is the Hebrew noun *shave'*, which means "vanity, nothingness, or emptiness." So another way of translating this commandment is "You shall not carry the name of the LORD your God in emptiness." Or more succinctly, "You shall not mis-carry the name of the LORD your God."

If the message we're communicating and the message we'd like to be communicating aren't the same, there's a gap. And we must close that gap, because we carry the name of God, and we've been asked to carry it well—to accurately convey to the world what God is like in how we live. We are the message. We are walking billboards for God. We serve as His priests, and we wear the color blue. And whether we like it or not, people will take their cues about how to live from you and me. If we don't live well, we can give the wrong message about God and lead others astray.

Like Samson.

As a Nazirite, he was called to epitomize a lifestyle wholly in sync to the will of God. He was called to put on display the essence of who God was. He was called to see and interact with the world through a blue filter. Tragically, his eyes rarely contained a pigment of blue. He chose to do what was right in his own eyes, and his eyes led him astray. Consequently, his eyes led many others astray as well. His own people lost sight of that blue and tragedy after tragedy ensued—each the result of the nation of Israel failing to have blue in their eyes. Samson was not the message he was called to be, and it cost him and others dearly.

As we endeavor to live into our identity of being priests of God, we would be well served to emulate the One who most exemplified and embodied being a priest of God—Jesus Christ. The writer of Hebrews uses the language of Jesus being a "high priest" through-out the letter[26] in connection with several facets of functionality. Notice the facet highlighted in Hebrews 4:

Therefore, since we have a great high priest who has ascended into heaven, Jesus the Son of God, let us hold firmly to the faith we pro-fess. For we do not have a high priest who is unable to empathize with our weaknesses, but we have one who has been tempted in every way, just as we are—yet he did not sin. (vv. 14–15)

As "priests" of the living God, we look to our "high priest," and we model our lives after the example He set. Every aspect of Jesus' life was attuned to the will of God. He set His eyes on the things of God, and literally became the hands and feet of God here on earth. Jesus saw His calling through the color blue.

In order to live into our true humanity, we must do the same. We must orient our eyes to the things of God and our calling in the world. We must shift our eyes away from our selfish desires and thinking our decisions don't matter. We must perceive that others will follow our lead, and we need to live a life worth imitating. We must see that we are the message of God, and we are to communicate it accurately.

But in order to do this well, we must see through a hue of blue, which means we gotta have blue eyes.

CHAPTER 7

Give Us What You've Got

So far, we've looked at all the ways Samson abused his gifts and got things wrong. But ultimately, we need to address the purpose for which his gifts were given in the first place. Samson's primary gift is unparalleled human strength. Yet as we've explored, his Nazirite vow precludes him from using his strength to kill. So the question we must seek to answer is, "Why did God give Samson superhuman strength if he's not allowed to kill?"

As with all challenging questions, you've got to come at this one from different angles in order to see how the pieces fit together. And let me acknowledge up front, there is no way of knowing for certain why Samson was given his gift of strength, and the purpose for which he was to steward it. God never outlines the details and intent. So what we're about to explore is a bit speculative. However, in light of this reality, I believe a plausible purpose emerges with respect to Samson's calling, because our gifts are always linked to our calling.

According to Judges 13:5, the angel of the Lord says to Manoah's wife, "...you shall conceive and give birth to a son, and no razor shall come upon his head, for the boy shall be a Nazirite to God from the womb; and he shall begin to deliver Israel from the hands of the Philistines" (NASB).

Samson's calling is twofold. One, he is to be a Nazirite, dedicated from the womb to serve the LORD wholeheartedly, and in the process set an example for his fellow Israelites of what a sold-out lifestyle for God looks like. And two, he is to begin to deliver the Israelites from the hands of the Philistines.[1] We've already addressed the first part of Samson's calling in the preceding chapters. It's the second half of Samson's calling that will drive our conversation for this chapter. Samson is called to address the oppression of the Philistines.

This isn't the first time the Philistines show up in the book of Judges. They show up momentarily in Judges 3 in the narrative of Shamgar, one of the Minor Judges. They're also mentioned in the Jephthah narrative in Judges 10. However, when they're reintroduced in Judges 13, we're quickly made aware they're a force to be reckoned with. The Samson narrative begins with the background detail that "again the Israelites did evil in the eyes of the LORD, so the LORD delivered them into the hands of the Philistines for forty years" (Judg. 13:1). Israel has been under the boot of the Philistines for forty years. This is the longest length of oppression preceding any judge in the book of Judges. In fact, it's twice as long as the next longest, telling us something of the strength of these people, and the gravity of the situation. Since Samson is called to begin dealing with the oppression of these Philistines, it's critical we understand who these Philistines are, where they come from, and what affinity Samson's gifts may have to their way of life.

Philistine Origins

The Philistines are a fascinating group of people. They aren't native to the land of Canaan. In fact, they came into the land around the same time as the Israelites, or perhaps a couple of hundred years later if one takes the early date for the Exodus.[2] What we know from historical sources is that the Philistines were part of a larger group of people known as the Sea Peoples. According to Amos 9:7, the Philistines came from Caphtor (Crete). This corresponds with the archaeological and extrabiblical literary sources, which also indicate that the Sea People's homeland stretched into the Aegean, in the area of the Greek Isles. According to the evidence, in the late thirteenth and early twelfth centuries BC, the Sea Peoples went on a rampage all over the Mediterranean Basin, wreaking havoc and attacking the kingdoms in those lands.

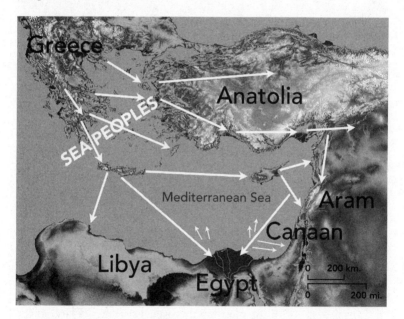

One of the kingdoms they attacked was Egypt, and a great battle took place in the Nile Delta in 1174 BC. We know about this famous battle because it's recorded in the annals of Ramesses III (ruled 1184–1153 BC), which he inscribed on one of the walls of his mortuary temple, known as Medinet Habu, located in the modern Egyptian city of Luxor (ancient Thebes). On the wall, the battle is shown, and in good pharaonic fashion, Ramesses III portrays himself and his army crushing the Sea Peoples. However, the evidence seems to indicate Ramesses III was more about propaganda than the truth, because following the battle, a subgroup of the Sea Peoples—the Philistines—settled along the southwestern coast of the land of Canaan, which eventually became known as Philistia.

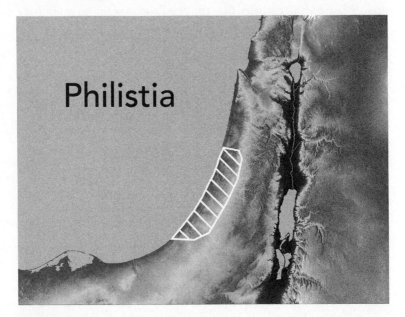

What these Philistines did was telling. One didn't haphazardly take up residence on the southwestern coast of the land of Canaan. The land of Canaan was one of the most highly coveted stretches of land in the ancient world because of its strategic location. The southwestern coast, where the Philistines established themselves, was among the most valuable real estate within the land of Canaan, owing to its climate, ease of travel, quality of crops, and interconnectedness. The main international coastal highway went right through the heart of this land. So it was not some virgin territory the Philistines decided to inhabit.

What's more, prior to the Philistines' arrival, the Egyptians had been ruling Canaan for more than three hundred years. So in all likelihood, when the Sea Peoples attacked the Egyptians, the Egyptians didn't crush them. Either the battle was a stalemate, or the Sea Peoples won but knew it would be too difficult to get into the heart of Egypt and ultimately take over the kingdom. Therefore, a group among them chose to settle along the southwestern coast of Canaan, knowing full well the Egyptians did not have the military strength to keep them from doing so.

If Egypt had won the battle in the Nile Delta in the fashion Ramesses III claims, and had the military strength to maintain their presence in the land of Canaan—an area they had been controlling for hundreds of years—there's no way the Philistines would have ended up on the coast of Canaan and establishing their five main cities, which dominated the landscape. They took it away from Egypt. The Philistines were a force to be reckoned with.[3]

Additionally, we know from the biblical and extrabiblical literary sources, along with the archaeological evidence, that the Philistines were a highly sophisticated and technologically advanced culture. So when we are told Samson is called to address the Philistines, this isn't some chump group in the land. They are a powerful force, and they have had the upper hand on the Israelites for the last forty years. Samson's calling is a big one.

A Possible Olympic Heritage

We know the Philistines are, in part, from the Greek Isles, which means they may have been, in part, Greeks. As with all cultures, there are certain values, customs, and lifestyles that define them. This system of the ancient Greeks is known as Hellenism. Although there is currently no archaeological evidence to clearly support a connection between the Philistines and later Greek Hellenism, the close proximity of these two cultures means the possibility cannot be ruled out. What's more, the lack of archaeological finds does not prove the absence of a connection. There always exists the possibility of a "what if." What if thirty years from now, a hundred years from now, archaeologists discover hard evidence of a connection between the Philistines and the ancient Greeks? Then, Samson's calling to the Philistines and his particular gifts would make sense in light of the Greek appreciation of feats of strength and agility.

Among the many aspects of Hellenism was the appreciation of and emphasis upon the human body. According to Hellenism, the greatest source of beauty was the human body. Therefore, an enormous value was placed on the human body—what it looked like and what it could do. This led to nudity playing a pivotal role in Greek culture because a good Greek would never want to perpetually cover up the most exquisite form of beauty. At least that's how they reasoned. And when it came to performance, what the human body could accomplish drove the culture. The Greeks loved their athletics, and sports became paramount. With their values of sports and nudity, it's no wonder the athletic contests were performed in the nude because it was the natural bridging of beauty and performance.

It was the Greeks' great love for athletics that eventually led to the creation of the Olympic Games, the world's greatest stage for athletic contests, both then and now. It's commonly held that the Games were inaugurated in 776 BC. However, archaeological evidence from Olympia, where the Games began, suggests athletic contests were happening there as early as the late eleventh century BC.[4] That puts the beginning of these contests and the battle between the Sea Peoples and the Egyptians within roughly a hundred-and-fifty-year window.

Although that's a considerable gap in time, there are a couple of possibilities to keep in mind. The Philistine migrations do not appear to be a singular event. They seemed to have happened over a period of time. Thus, there is the possibility that the Philistine migrations could have continued into the period during which the games were being formulated, and these later Philistine immigrants brought the same appreciation of athleticism with them to Philistia. Another possibility is that by the time of Samson's struggles with the Philistines, which were taking place around the time the athletic contests were under way at Olympia, the Philistines might have been hearing reports from their Aegean cousins about athletic contests being devoted to the gods. Both of these possibilities suggest the Philistines may have emerged from, or had ties to, this athletic-crazed Greek culture, and all the facets that went along with it.

Once such facet was the worship of the gods. The Olympics began as a festival to their head deity, Zeus. So from their inception, the Olympic Games were connected to the gods. The people believed that the athletes' stamina, strength, speed, and agility were gifts from the gods. Thus, when an athlete won an event, they were praised, but even more so the athlete's patron deity was praised for giving the athlete the ability to do what they did. This mind-set—that the gods were behind the gifts of the athletes—played itself out not only on the athletic field, but also on the battlefield. The gods gave the warriors the physical abilities to conquer their enemies.

We clearly see this belief system playing out in the biblical text in 1 Samuel 17, which recounts the infamous story of David and Goliath. Roughly fifty to sixty years after Samson's death, the Philistines are again wreaking havoc in the land. This time they're seeking to get up into the hill country through the Elah Valley, which is the valley just south of the Sorek Valley, where much of the Samson story takes place. The Philistines are occupying the south side of the valley, and the Israelites, the north side. Goliath, the champion of the Philistines, stands up and shouts a challenge to the Israelites, in which he includes the statement "This day I defy the armies of Israel!" (1 Sam. 17:10).

Perceptively, David interprets his statement to mean he's defying God. For David asks a bit later in the story, "What will be done for the man who kills this Philistine and removes this disgrace from Israel? Who is this uncircumcised Philistine that he should defy the armies of the living God?" (1 Sam. 17:26). David repeats this claim to Saul when he states, "Your servant has killed both the lion and the bear; this uncircumcised Philistine will be like one of them, because he has defied the armies of the living God" (1 Sam. 17:36).

In the event we wonder if David is reading too much into Goliath's statement, the exchange between Goliath and David removes any such wonderings. After Goliath looks David over, he says to him, "Am I a dog, that you come at me with sticks?" The writer then tells us, "And the Philistine cursed David by his gods" (1 Sam. 17:43). To which David counters, "You come against me with sword and spear and javelin, but I come against you in the name of the LORD Almighty, the God of the armies of Israel, whom you have defied" (1 Sam. 17:45).

What David and Goliath both believe is that it's never simply warrior versus warrior, or army versus army. It's deity versus deity. Behind the warriors and the armies are the deities who empower them, and therefore, what you do says something about your god (or gods).

This is again why Samson ends up in the temple of Dagon following his subjugation, because Dagon was the patron deity of the Philistines. And this is why the Philistines praise Dagon for his victory over their nemesis, Samson, and his god. Even though it was Delilah's ruse that eventually did Samson in, the Philistines believed it was Dagon who defeated not only Samson but God as well.

All of this matters because Samson's gift is strength. His body is able to do things the Philistines have never seen done before. And the Philistines are perplexed by these abilities—from the perspective of not only what he's capable of doing, but how he even has the capacity to do it. Notice again why Delilah is employed. According to the narrative, "The rulers of the Philistines went to her and said, 'See if you can lure him into showing you the secret of his great strength and how we can overpower him so we may tie him up and subdue him. Each one of us will give you eleven hundred shekels of silver'" (Judg. 16:5).

They agree to pay her sixteen and a half million dollars to figure out the source of his strength. Which tells us there is nothing about the appearance or physique of Samson that indicates he should be able to do what he does. Remember, these Philistines are not primitive and barbaric people who can't tell their left hands from their right. They are a highly sophisticated and technologically advanced people. The fact that they can't identify the source of his strength tells us Samson's appearance is not one of a bodybuilder. He's not six foot seven, three hundred pounds, with muscles bulging all over the place, as nearly every film or television show on the life of Samson depicts. If Samson had this physique, then the Philistines would know the source of his great strength—his muscles![5] But this isn't the case. Samson's a normal-looking dude, and yet what he's able to do is anything but normal.

I'm willing to bet the Philistines are mesmerized by Samson's athletic abilities.[6] Granted, they're furious with what he's doing because they're suffering as a result of it. But what he's able to do is overwhelmingly impressive to them, especially if they are indeed a culture that celebrates the achievements of the human body. Thus, Samson's gift of strength may have had glorious affinity to what the Philistines valued.

Think about the implications of this.

Imagine the potential if Samson had used his abilities to capture their attention in a redemptive way, rather than in a violent one.

Imagine the impact if Samson, knowing full well the Philistines loved their athletics, had ventured over to the coastal plain and jumped into the athletic contests the Philistines were possibly holding in their spare time (wearing at least a loincloth, of course[7]).

Imagine the response if Samson would've competed in their foot races, wrestling matches, and javelin-throwing, accomplishing feats they'd never seen done before.

Understand, it wouldn't have mattered to them if Samson was a foreigner or whether they initially liked him or not. If an NBA player came out and hit his first twenty-five shots in a game, any lover of basketball would be overwhelmingly flabbergasted, even if they didn't care for the player who did it. Or if a sprinter ran the hundred-meter dash in 9.4 seconds, anyone who appreciates human speed would be speechless, whether they liked the runner's attitude or not. This is because there's a certain appreciation that comes when your expectations of the possible are throttled in the arenas of what you value.

And imagine if, when they asked him how he was able to do what he was doing, Samson said, "Let me tell you about the one true God who has given me the ability to do what I'm able to do, even though I don't have the physical stature to do it. Let me tell you about the creator of the universe, and the kind of power He wields. Let me tell you about what this God is like and what His hopes and goals are for the world. And let me tell you how He desires for you to be part of them."

Samson would've had the credibility. He would've had the platform. He would've had the voice. The Philistines were most certainly speculating about the deity behind Samson's physical abilities.

Samson needed then only to highlight the God behind the gift, and by doing so, he could've leveraged his abilities to compel the Philistines to follow God.

This is what I believe Samson was called to do. This is what makes sense in light of his abilities, and the history and culture of the people whom Samson was to address. Samson was called to use his gifts for the glory of God. He was called to use them to further God's hopes and dreams for the world. He was called to use his unique talents to address those who didn't care about God, and to do so in a redemptive, nonviolent way.

Now Us

What was true of Samson is true of us all. We all have gifts and abilities. Whether our gifts are as impressive as Samson's or not, we are called to use them in the arenas where God has placed us to further His purposes. God has big plans for the world, and ever since the beginning of human history, God has been looking for people to join Him in His redemptive cause of restoring the world.

We all wrestle with knowing what we're supposed to do. We all desire to do something significant in the world: to leave our mark. We all want to believe we were put here for a purpose. Some of us know what we've been created to do. Others of us have been searching for that answer all our lives. And there's an undercurrent of fear. A fear that we'll never figure it out, or worse, we've missed it. Or maybe for some of us, we know what we're supposed to do, but we're scared to do it. Whatever it may be, we all struggle from time to time with knowing what we're supposed do.

And let's be honest. Looking at Samson's calling can be a bit maddening. An angel comes to his mother and says, "He is to be a Nazirite and he is to begin delivering the people from the Philistines." Seems pretty straightforward. Imagine if your calling was that clear. What if an angel came to your mother and father and said, "Your child is to be an elementary school teacher." Or "a nurse." "A musician." "An engineer." Think of all the time, money, and worry it would've saved you.

But despite the lack of overt clarity many of us have, we're here for a purpose. And it's our responsibility to figure it out. So how do we do that? Let's begin with one of my favorite rabbinic stories.

A rabbi is heading home one evening. It's getting dark, and the path he's on has a fork in the road. The natural bend of the path goes to the right. However, for the rabbi to get home, he must veer to the left. Absorbed in his Scripture reciting, he continues to the right, missing his turn. Unaware of his error, he continues on until out of the darkness he hears shouted, "Who are you? What are you doing here?" Startled by these words, and the realization he's stumbled upon a Roman military outpost, the rabbi suddenly stops. Once more, the Roman soldier shouts, "Who are you? What are you doing here?" The rabbi thinks for a few moments. And then in good rabbinic fashion, the rabbi responds with a question. "How much do you get paid a day?" Perplexed by the rabbi's response, the soldier replies, "I get paid two denarii a day, Jew. Why?" And the rabbi responds, "Because I'll double your wage if you'll come to my house every morning and ask me those same two questions."

Who are you?

What are you doing here?

These are two of the most important questions we can ask. And they are two of the most difficult questions to answer. They are questions of identity and purpose. And in that order. If we're going to understand what we're supposed to do, we must first understand who we are.

Who Are You?

Within the first week of my becoming a pastor at Central, our church held what we called a "Sacred Gathering." It was a two-hour prayer event that nearly five hundred people, mostly from our church, attended. As a community, we wanted to join together and lift not only our community up in prayer, but also our country and our world. The event took place a week before elections and during the time when Hurricane Sandy was wreaking destruction on the East Coast. Additionally, our church was also in a pivotal time of transition. Needless to say, there was much to pray about.

After a time of singing and small group prayer, we entered into a forty-minute space, which I would imagine for most was the most transforming part of the evening. We had several "stations" positioned on and around our stage, each facilitating an experience. We had a Confession station, consisting of low plastic bins filled with sand where individuals "wrote" their sins in the sand and, after confessing them before God, wiped them away. We had a Prayer station, where people could come and be joined by one of our pastors in prayer. We had an Attributes station, where individuals could come and write an attribute of God on a large piece of paper to remind themselves and others of the kind of God we serve. We had a Meditation station, consisting of a beautifully decorated cross and baskets around the periphery, which held slips of paper each with a passage about Jesus and a question to meditate upon. There was a Communion station, where people could take bread and dip it into a cup and partake of the Lord's Supper. There was also a Salvation station, where people could come and write on a giant board the names of friends and family who didn't know Christ, and of whom they were desperately praying for. It was startling how quickly that board filled up.

During the first twenty minutes I had the opportunity of

experiencing these stations before I was responsible for manning one. Every station I visited provided a meaningful experience. But it was the station that visited me that gave me the most transforming moment of the night. I was standing next to a group of people at the Meditation station, gazing upon the decorated cross. Emerging from the crowd to my left was a man I hadn't seen before. This wasn't shocking since I'd been part of this community for only a week. It didn't even dawn upon me he was heading my way until I saw his outstretched hand holding a piece of bread, and a look that said, "It's for you."

He was obviously coming from the Encouragement station—obvious to me, but not to you since you haven't been privy to this final station. The Encouragement station was at the very center of the stage. It contained a plump loaf of bread atop a tall, circular table. The instructions were simple: "Pluck a piece from the loaf, find someone to give it to, and upon giving it to them, say a word of blessing or prayer over them."

I was immediately fond of Steve because his appearance reminded me of the late Dwight Pryor—a phenomenal Bible scholar who played a pivotal role in my life.[8] Handing me the piece of bread, Steve said: "Brad, welcome to Central. We're glad you're here. May you always remain faithful. May you boldly teach the word of God with great power and conviction. And may you remain you. Continue to be who God has called you to be. Don't be somebody else. Just be you."

Don't be somebody else. Just be you.

I believe these are some of the most instructive words we can hear. Because sometimes I find the hardest person to be is yourself. If I were to ask you what you appreciate most about yourself, you'd likely highlight a number of things, but it would take you some time. But if I asked you what you didn't like about yourself, I'm guessing you'd rattle off a list in no time. We've been conditioned to notice what's wrong with us long before we appreciate what's right with us.

We live in a culture where we encounter some three thousand advertisements a day, promoting products that will make right what's wrong with us. Without these products, we're apparently incomplete and lacking. We're told in the magazine sections of the checkout lanes that we're not smart enough, fit enough, or sexy enough. Everywhere we look, who we are is brought into question.

Over time the constant bombardment of these messages begins skewing our perception of reality and of ourselves. I've heard it takes the average person thirty-five years to accept who they are. That's a long time. As a result, we often spend an unhealthy amount of time, energy, and finances trying to correct what's wrong with us, or seeking to become someone else, altogether abandoning who we are. And oftentimes, we don't even realize we're doing it.

I know that's been true in my life.

When I first began preaching, I taught and sounded a lot like my mentors. I exhibited a similar persona. I navigated the teaching platform with similar movements. I worked through a teaching with a similar pacing. I verbalized my points with ridiculously similar tonal inflections. I motioned my hands with the same gestures. Everything I did was patterned after what I had observed and learned from my mentors. They were masters at what they did. They were the best I'd seen, and I wanted to do what they did. Or perhaps more truthfully, I wanted to be just like them.

I would imagine this is true of us all. We all have people we look up to. Some would even go so far as to call them "heroes." Ironically, some of the people we admire we don't even know. For all we know, they could be jerks behind the cameras or off the stage, but we admire at least the side we're privy to. And what we admire we seek to imitate. Oftentimes it means wearing the same clothes, drinking the same coffee, listening to the same music, toting the same bag, or even sounding just like them.

I remember after one teaching, a gentleman approached me and remarked, "Wow, you sound more like so-and-so than so-and-so sounds like himself." "Thanks, I guess" was all I could muster. It was intended as a compliment, but it felt more like an indictment. I wasn't being me, and this was the first time I was confronted with this reality. Looking back, I needed that moment more than I could've imagined. I needed to be set free from the pursuit of being someone else. I had to recognize that God created me to be me.

The same goes for you as well.

Granted, there are certain habits and characteristics others exemplify that are healthy for us to instill in our own lives. But we must be careful that in the process of adopting, we don't become more like them and less like us. We must fight against our propensity to become someone else.

I can't be someone else, and neither can you. You need to be you. You don't need to be them. We don't need another one of them. We need a first edition of you. You have a voice. We need your voice. Learn from others what you need to learn, but implement into "you" the things that will help "you" become a better "you." God has created you as a unique individual and desires that you become all He has created you to be, for your benefit and His glory. In order to be who God has created you to be, you've got to live into "you."

And you must know up front that you are loved and accepted the way you are. This pursuit of being you has nothing to do with earning or achieving. There's this amazing moment in Jesus' life that has been richly meaningful to me. It comes at His baptism. As Matthew records it: "As soon as Jesus was baptized, he went up out of the water. At that moment heaven was opened, and he saw the Spirit of God descending like a dove and alighting on him. And a voice from heaven said, 'This is my Son, whom I love; with him I am well pleased'" (Matt. 3:16–17).

These are significant words of love and affirmation. But what makes this moment so powerful is where it comes in the storyline. Jesus' baptism is at the front end of His ministry. According to the gospel writers, Jesus hasn't done anything yet.[9] He hasn't given a monumental sermon. He hasn't forgiven anyone's sins. He hasn't healed any illness. He hasn't walked on water. He hasn't driven out any demons. He hasn't raised anyone from the dead. His list of accomplishments is empty. And yet it's precisely at this moment that God proclaims these words of a proud parent: "This is my Son, whom I love; with him I am well pleased."

God loves you. Period. It has been said time and again, there's nothing you can do to make God love you any more, and there's nothing you can do to make God love you any less. God loves you because you're you. He doesn't love you because of where you were born, or what your education level is, or who your parents are, or what you have or have not done. He doesn't love you for who you're going to be or what you're going to do. God loves you because He made you. You were created by God, made in His image, and clothed with glory and honor.[10] That's where your value lies.

When we know we're loved and accepted, we're set free to become who we need to be, not in order to be loved and accepted, but because we already are. Our identity is set. We don't need to impress. We can simply be who we were designed to be, in order to do what we've been called to do, because we do have a purpose. We all have a job to do. And it is our responsibility to discern and figure out what it is and do it. And we've got to be true to who we are and the gifts we've been given. As Steven Pressfield so poignantly puts it:

We're not born with unlimited choices. We can't be anything we want to be. We come into this world with a specific, personal destiny. We have a job to do, a calling to enact, a self to become. We are who we are from the cradle, and we're stuck with it. Our job in this lifetime is not to shape ourselves into some ideal we imagine we ought to be, but to find out who we already are and become it.[11]

What Are You Doing Here?

To understand the nature of this question, it's helpful to think about it through the lens of these other questions as well:

Are you stewarding your life well?

Are you being true to yourself?

Are you doing what you're called to be doing?

Are you maximizing the gifts you've been given?

Are you holding back in any way?

One of the more penetrating quotes I often reflect upon comes from the German author Johann Wolfgang von Goethe. He said, "Hell begins the day God grants you the vision to see all that you could have done, should have done, and would have done, but did not do."

Nobody wants to live with regrets. We all want to do what we've been designed to do. It's why as a pastor, I'm often asked, "How do I know what I'm supposed to do?" We've all had this question. It's a question about our individual callings. This is an important distinction to make. Up to this point in the book, we've been exploring our universal callings as fellow human beings who live life well. What it means to live a life of service and humility. What it means to listen to the voice of the Spirit and respond. What it looks like to forgive others, and set a positive example for others to follow. But this question gets us into our specific callings—what we've each been called to do, like what we explored with Samson in this chapter.

What I'd like to offer are some thoughts and suggestions to help guide you in your pursuit of your specific callings. This is not the be-all and end-all approach, and it's definitely not a complete guide.

It's a conversation starter. It's intended to help get the wheels moving and provide you with some things to think about and wrestle through.[12]

To begin, I'd recommend answering a series of questions:

What do you think you're called to do?

What are your gifts?

What are you passionate about?

What's your greatest hurt?[13]

What are the things you love to do?

What gives you the most joy?

What are the things you currently do that if you stopped doing them you would spontaneously combust?

If you could do anything, what would it be?

These are simple questions, and yet they're revealing. As you unpack your answers, a common theme may begin to emerge, giving you a sense of direction on where you should go. Even if there isn't a clear theme, you likely have some ideas on what would be worth pursuing.

It's worth noting you won't likely have a eureka moment figuring out your calling or knowing what you're supposed to do. In fact, for the vast majority of people, gaining clarity on one's calling or knowing what to do is a process—it's a journey. And this is probably the most important thing to understand. Life and one's calling are a journey, not a destination. It's about the journey and the process, because it is here where we're shaped and formed. It is here where we learn to rely upon God. God is a God of the journey and not the destination. It's in the journey where you understand who God is and what you're called to do. And it happens over time.

The idea of this being a process is hard for many to swallow. We are a people who want to know what's ahead. We want the answers now. We are an instant culture. We're used to getting what we want, and when we want it. We are used to having control.

I remember when we moved back from Israel. We had subleased our condo to some college students (who actually did a remarkable job of taking care of the place—who would've thought?). Since they were college students, and needed to be responsible with what little money they did have, they decided not to continue the cable service we had while we were gone. So upon our return, I called the cable company and requested to have our cable reactivated and updated. Two days later, a technician showed up and installed a new cable box, which came with a new remote. This upgrade now included DVR—Digital Video Recorder. I would imagine most of you are familiar with this, but to the uninitiated, DVR allows you to pause and rewind live television. It also allows you the ability to digitally record television shows you're not at home to watch. This is by far the greatest feature because you can watch a sixty-minute show in forty minutes, and not have to deal with the annoyance of commercials. It's quite an amazing technological advancement.

But here's the problem with DVR. It gives us greater control over that which we didn't have control over before. Prior to DVR, if you wanted to watch a show, you had to program VCR or be at home in front of the television to watch it. That's all changed. Television used to control us, but now we're able to control it (for the most part). DVR isn't inherently bad or evil. But what DVR, and virtually every new technology, does is give us more control than what we had before. And the more control we get, the more we expect it. Which makes life very frustrating for most of us, because life doesn't lend us the same kind of control the cable companies do. And this often manifests itself with our callings. We get frustrated when we don't have things all figured out. Listen, if you don't exactly know what you're supposed to do, that's okay. It's a process that takes time.

I remember having breakfast one morning with my friend Ray. We were sitting in a corner booth awaiting our food, and I was venting about my lack of clarity on the direction of my calling. I was a year through seminary, and I still didn't know what I wanted to do. I knew I wanted to teach the Bible, but as for in what setting and in what position, I was clueless. I specifically remember saying in a hyperventilating kind of way, "Ray, I don't know if I want to be a senior pastor, an associate pastor, a teaching pastor, a seminary professor, a college professor, a high school teacher, whether I'm supposed to lead biblical study trips to the Middle East, or do something else." Ray calmly looked at me and said, "Slow down. Breathe for a moment. You don't have to have everything figured out right now. Just tell me, what do you believe you're called to do?"

Without hesitation, I said, "I believe I'm called to teach the Bible." To which he immediately remarked, "Then your job is to become the best teacher you can be, and let God figure out where your teachings get channeled to."

That advice changed me.

I was so concerned about the future I wasn't maximizing the present. From that point forward, I didn't worry or focus on what I would ultimately do. I let go of the destination and focused on being the best teacher I could be, and trusted that God would reveal in due time where my teachings would go, or what position I would hold. I simply focused on the next step.

It's all about the next step. This is what it means to have a journey mind-set. This is what it means to journey well. The answer we might be looking for may be a thousand steps down the road. But in order to get there, we must take it one step at a time. Our responsibility is not the destination, but the next step. And this involves action.

Which leads me to something my good friend George says to me all the time: "Give God something to bless." So often we sit back on our hands waiting for God to show us the way. But over and over again in the Scriptures, God challenges His people to make the first move. God wants us to take the first step. God wants us to give Him something to work with. Jesus demonstrated this time and again. He didn't feed the five thousand with nothing. He took five small loaves and two fish, and did something miraculous with them. This is what God wants us to do. He wants us to offer what we can and trust that He'll make it what it needs to be, or show us a different way. But we have to take the first step.

Along the same lines, something George also taught me was to never say "no" until God says "no." Recently, I lobbed this advice at a guy who contacted me about attending one of the biblical study trips I lead to the Middle East. He said he really wanted to go, but didn't feel like God wanted him to. Since I didn't know him, I was hesitant about being frank with him like I would be with someone I knew. But I really liked this guy, and felt this trip would greatly benefit him, so I pressed him by asking, "How do you know God doesn't want you to go? You clearly have a desire to go. Why would God not want you to have an incredible two-week experience, walking the land of the Bible, and learning the Scriptures in ways that could shape your life forever?" He said, "Because I don't have the finances to go." I replied, "Don't let that be the determining factor. Just because you don't have the money right now doesn't mean you're not supposed to go." I then went on to ask him, "What have you done to raise the necessary funds for this trip?" "Nothing," he replied. To which I replied, "God hasn't said, 'no,' you have."

I then walked him through the idea of not saying "no" until God says "no" and that he needed to give God something to bless. He immediately began talking to family and friends about his desire to have this experience, and whether anyone would be willing to help with the finances. About a week later, I got a call from him. "I'm supposed to go on this trip!" he said with excitement. He went on to tell me how several friends and family had contributed to his financial need. And in an unforeseen turn of events, a gentleman he didn't know well caught wind of his desire to go on the trip. He approached him and said, "You need to go on this trip. So how about I pay for half of it?"

This guy almost missed out on something his heart deeply desired because he assumed God had said "no" long before God ever said "no," and hadn't given God anything to bless. Now, God may not always say "yes." In fact, God may very well say "no." But at least give God the chance to say one way or the other. Whether it is taking a biblical study trip, applying for a new job, going back to school, trying out for a team, adopting a child, or whatever, don't make the mistake of saying "no" before God says "no." You may be missing out.

If you're thinking about trying something, take the next step. Make the call. Try it out. Get an interview. Apply for the internship. Check out the program. Volunteer to see how things work. Take a class. Have a conversation. Join the group. Take the risk. How else will you know if you don't give it a go? Give God something to work with, and see what happens. Then take the next step after that.

And don't get hung up on whether your calling is big and grandiose. There's a misconception that what we do has to be on a large scale. It doesn't. Your calling may not be to lead an organization, or to serve in Africa, or to find a cure for cancer. That doesn't make your calling any less important or compelling. What matters is that you do what you've been called to do, and you do it to the best of your ability. That's what's compelling.

My wife and I recently went to Bed Bath & Beyond to get a blender. I hate shopping for items like this. I'd rather watch paint dry, or sit through a T-ball game (that my kid's not playing in, of course). But since it was for the purpose of my breakfast shake, I had a vested interest. While we were perusing the blender aisle, a woman from the store greeted us and asked if we had any questions. We inquired about the differences between the makes and models. It was a boring request, which probably warranted a boring answer.

Not with her. Immediately her eyes lit up. For the next ten minutes, she gave an enthusiastic clinic on each of the blenders before us. QVC had nothing on her. We knew which one could pulverize an orange in the shortest amount of time. We knew which one had the strongest motor and would utilize the least amount of energy. We knew which one had the strongest ratings, and which ones were on the rise. She even shared with us what happened at the latest blender conference she attended, and what the authorities were saying about the various brands.

And so here I am, standing in a store I don't want to be in, listening to information about blenders, and yet I'm riveted. It was obvious this woman was doing what she was called to do. She was made to help people make decisions on everyday household items. And not only did she do it with great enthusiasm and competency, but she loved doing it. What she did was compelling, and it impacted us.

You don't have to do something extravagant to be compelling. Some of the most compelling aspects of life happen in the everyday, humdrum activities and relationships. From time to time, my wife, who is a stay-at-home mom, will tell me she doesn't feel she's doing enough or living a compelling enough life. I gently remind her that she's doing more than enough, and that she's an amazing mother. And that's compelling. In a world of broken households, one of the most compelling things you can do is be a great mother, or a great father. In a world where more than half of all marriages end in divorce, one of the most compelling things you can do is have a thriving marriage. In a world where people move so fast they hardly have time to sleep, spending time mentoring a child is compelling.

A final thought about callings is that they may change or morph over time. We may be doing something today that's within our calling that we may not do in the future. For many of us, there are seasons for what we do. If you're a stay-at-home mother, you won't always be a stay-at-home mother. What your world consists of now is changing diapers, and putting away toys, and giving time-outs, and going to soccer practice, and attending dance recitals, and taking late showers (if you get one at all), and getting everyone ready for school without pulling out your hair or theirs. But it won't always be this way. You won't always be doing this. Although you'll always be a mother (because once a mother, always a mother, right?), your life will likely change when you become an empty nester. You may enter into a career you've never dreamt of, or you'll enter into the career you've been longing to do. But for the time being, perhaps this is where your energy is to be channeled. Focus on how you can do it well, knowing it's for a specific period of time, and that other opportunities will come later.

Leveraging Our Gifts

Whether you've identified your calling and you're living it out, or you're still trying to figure things out, we've all been given gifts we're using in one way or another. So allow me to conclude this chapter by offering three ways we ought to be leveraging our gifts, irrespective of whether we're certain on our callings yet or not.

One, we leverage our gifts for God's glory. Our gifts first and foremost are not about us. They're about God. It is He who has given them, and it is He who wishes to be honored through them. Our gifts were not given to further our own agenda. They were given to further His. This is where Samson got it wrong. He leveraged his gifts for his personal glory, and robbed God of what was due Him. When we are successful in what we do, and people praise us for our accomplishments, we must find ways to put the giver of our gifts on display for others to see. It can't be about us. Jesus implored, "Let your light shine before others, that they may see your good deeds and glorify your Father in heaven" (Matt. 5:16). The focus must move from us to God.

Two, we leverage our gifts for the benefit of others and for our world. When Jesus was asked, "What's the greatest commandment?" He responded by saying we ought to love God and love others (see Matt. 22:34–40). Love of God is a natural extension into loving others. As we've explored, this is something Samson chose not to live into. He didn't love others well because he didn't serve anyone other than himself. That's not true living. In fact, that's a lonely and miserable experience. We have a responsibility to one another. We're called to serve one another with the gifts we've been given. We love well by serving, and we serve well by leveraging our gifts for the betterment of others.

And third, we leverage our gifts for our joy. I've heard it said, "God is most glorified in us when we are most satisfied in Him."[14] To be satisfied is to have joy. We are called to pursue joy in everything we do. Yes, our gifts are not about us, but they've been given for our enjoyment. God wants us to have joy in the talents we have, and in the work He's given us to do. To be a follower of Jesus isn't to be stripped of fun and joy. Quite the opposite. When we truly understand who we are in Jesus Christ, and what we've been designed to do, there is a perennial spring of joy that not only waters our lives, but spills over and nourishes others' lives as well. So be thankful for what you have. Find delight in what you have before you, even if you're in process.

We all want the world to change, but it requires each of us playing our part. So figure out your part. Recognize that your job is the relentless pursuit of who God has called you to be. We need you to be who God has created you to be. And we need you to do what God has called you to do. So be you. Please be you. Do what you've been gifted to do, and do it to the best of your ability. Don't let excuses get in the way. Don't hide behind the risk. Don't give way to fear. Don't hold back. Don't rob us of your gift. Give us what you've got.

CHAPTER 8

Hope for Faulty People

Did you know that Samson shows up in the New Testament?
It's only once but it's significant.

Hebrews 11 is often referred to as the "Faith Hall of Fame," or simply the "Hall of Faith." It's one of the most compelling chapters in the entire New Testament. It begins by stating, "Now faith is confidence in what we hope for and assurance about what we do not see. This is what the ancients were commended for" (vv. 1–2). The rest of the chapter then highlights what great heroes of the faith from the Old Testament did, a list that includes Noah, Abraham, Sarah, Isaac, Jacob, Joseph, Moses, Rahab, and others. Their stories are recounted to encourage and challenge followers of God. It's an impressive list, and what gets commended about these individuals is remarkable.

Most of the characters listed you'd expect. That is, until you reach verse 32, which reads, "And what more shall I say? I do not have time to tell about Gideon, Barak, Samson and Jephthah..."

Wow. This is about as unexpected as getting caught in a snowstorm in the Sahara Desert. Based on everything we've covered, Samson shouldn't be on that list. Either we've missed something, and we need to go back to the drawing board, or this passage opens up a whole new vista on how to understand Samson's life.

I remember working through my Samson research and coming across this passage for the first time. I was dumbfounded. For the life of me, I couldn't understand why Samson was included on this list. It didn't make sense. He didn't belong in the company of such great heroes. But then I noticed whom Samson was listed alongside of—Gideon, Barak, and Jephthah, all characters from the book of Judges—and I realized Samson wasn't the only anomaly.

Gideon was tasked by God to deliver the Israelites from the hands of the Midianites and Amalekites. Though knowing the will of God, Gideon badgered God for a sign of confirmation, either demonstrating his lack of faith or his lack of desire to live out his calling. Once confirmed, Gideon did what he was asked to do, and did a commendable job. The Israelites defeated their oppressors, and there was peace in the land for forty years. However, Gideon dealt ruthlessly with two Israelite cities that didn't assist him and his men in their time of need. He also made an object of worship, from the spoils of war, which became a deadly snare to himself, his family, and to all of Israel.[1]

Barak was a powerful military commander in the northern part of the country, who was summoned by Deborah, Israel's judge at the time, to lead a battle against Sisera, the commander of the Canaanite forces. Barak refused the request, showing a decided lack of faith in God, until Deborah assured him that she'd join him. Putting his faith more in Deborah than in God, Barak lost the honor of subduing Sisera even though his army won the battle.[2]

Jephthah was a social outcast, the son of a prostitute, but a mighty warrior. When the Ammonites became a nuisance in the land, Jephthah was asked to lead the people against this commendable foe. A classic example of rising from the ashes, Jephthah accepted the role of commander and admirably lived into his responsibility. He led his people into battle and gained a glorious victory. But he made a vow that if God gave him victory over the Ammonites, he'd sacrifice the first thing that came out of his house to greet him. It was his daughter. He kept his vow, and burned his only child alive, not only doing what was reprehensible to God, but also sacrificing his family's future.[3]

All of a sudden, Samson doesn't look so bad, does he? Clearly, he isn't the only one on the list we should question. Gideon, Barak, and Jephthah all had greats flaws, just like Samson. And yet they're all listed. It makes you wonder if the writer of Hebrews got a little sidetracked and threw in names that actually belonged in a Hall of Failure. But the more you analyze the lives of those listed, and the lives of other significant characters in the Bible, the more you begin to recognize they all had faults and failures.

Adam and Eve ate the fruit.[4]

Cain killed his brother.[5]

Noah ended up drunk and naked.[6]

Abraham took matters into his own hands by having sex with his wife's servant, rather than waiting for God to provide him an heir through his own wife.[7] Oh yeah, and he lied about his wife being his sister. Not once but twice.[8]

Sarah lied to God's face.[9]

Isaac also lied about his wife being his sister.[10]

Jacob was a model citizen of deception (his name meant "deceiver"), who tricked his father into giving him his brother's blessing.[11] He also had twelve sons through two wives and two female servants.[12] His dysfunctional family of thirteen (don't forget about his daughter, Dinah) lived out stories of anger, jealousy, deception, betrayal, and murder.

Joseph was a cocky teenager, who enjoyed irritating the snot out of his brothers.[13]

Judah impregnated his daughter-in-law.[14]

Moses was a murderer.[15] And came up with every excuse not to do what God asked.[16] He finally conceded, only to get so fed up with the Israelites at the end of their desert journey that he made a decision that cost him entry into the Promised Land.[17]

Aaron fashioned a golden calf that magically leapt into existence (well, that's how he described it).[18]

Rahab was a prostitute.[19]

David committed not only adultery, but murder.[20] His family was a mess. Even though he was a man after God's own heart, he went to his deathbed handing Solomon, his son, a hit list.[21]

Solomon was a train wreck. After seven hundred wives and three hundred concubines (seriously, how does one even remember their names?), his heart was completely led astray. He did evil in the eyes of the LORD, and many would argue he was the worst king in Israelite history because the kingdom split following his reign.[22]

Elijah became so discouraged that he gave up and asked God to kill him.[23]

Jeremiah wanted to quit the moment he found out God wanted him to be a prophet.[24]

John the Baptist, the great forerunner to the ministry of Jesus, struggled with Jesus' messianic agenda.[25]

Jesus' twelve disciples argued about who would be the greatest among them immediately after Jesus told them he was going to die.[26]

Peter, one of the inner disciples and leader among the group, denied Jesus three times—even after he was told he would do so.[27]

Paul was a murderer, and single-handedly set out to destroy Jesus' followers before his path was redirected.[28]

And the list goes on and on and on...

Now, you may be thinking, "Yeah, but they did great things as well." And that's precisely the point. They did great things, and yet they also had great failings. And we are given both.

The Bible holds nothing back. It tells it like it is. It has no favorites, and it shows no partiality. No one is exempt from scrutiny. There are no sacred cows in the sacred Scriptures. Everyone's life, in all its goodness, rawness, and brokenness, is fair game for analysis and publication. Consequently, the Bible accentuates both the greatness and the weakness of humanity.

Because we're given both, we see that everyone had their struggles. No one had it all together. Some days they got things right. Other days they got things terribly wrong. They all had their flaws. They all had brokenness in their stories. And yet in spite of it all, God still chose to use them.

This is why I believe Samson shows up in Hebrews 11. Not because he was someone great, but because he was utilized by someone great. That's the point of Hebrews 11. Hebrews 11 is not about the greatness of humanity. It's about the goodness and grace of God to use broken and faulty people to accomplish His purposes, sometimes in collaboration with their efforts, and sometimes in spite of their efforts.

With Samson, we see the latter. In fact, there's a statement within the narrative that speaks directly to this, even though it seems problematic at first. After Samson demands that his parents obtain the Timnite woman as his wife, the narrator adds a parenthetical statement that reads, "His parents did not know that this was from the LORD, who was seeking an occasion to confront the Philistines; for at that time they were ruling over Israel" (Judg. 14:4). What's problematic is that it appears God's playing matchmaker, causing Samson to desire this Philistine woman. But it's illogical for God to make Samson break one of His own commandments—

namely, marrying a foreign woman in the land (which we discussed in Chapter 6). Here's how K. Lawson Younger Jr., a great scholar, explains it:

> [The LORD's] seeking does not imply that [He's] inciting Samson's lustful desire for the Timnite woman. Rather, it suggests that Samson's sinful actions accord with [the LORD's] will. God uses Samson in spite of his wrong motives and actions. From the following stories it becomes clear that left to himself, Samson would never have become involved in God's or even Israel's agenda. Left to themselves, the Israelites would have been satisfied to continue to coexist with the Philistines. But [the LORD] has other plans.[29]

Notably, every time Israel is oppressed in the book of Judges, they cry out to God—except now. When we're told at the beginning of the Samson narrative that the Philistines have been dominating Israel for forty years, there's nothing that follows. In every other instance, Israel cries out to God. But here, there's no cry for help. No pleading with God to raise up a judge. Nothing. They're content with having the Philistines rule over them. But God's not. Hence, Samson's calling. Yet as we've seen, Samson wasn't your model savior. He struggled. He joined the Israelite apathy to the point that God had to go looking for an occasion to confront the Philistines. He found one, and as Younger explained, God used Samson in spite of his wrong motives and actions to advance His purposes.

I do believe there were moments when God accomplished His purposes through Samson's willful collaboration, though. Keep in mind the vast majority of Samson's twenty-year rule isn't included in the narrative. We're given what we're given for the reason I discussed in Chapter 2—to help us see what a troubled life looks like and the effects thereof, so we don't repeat it. However, there was more to Samson's life than what we have recorded.

But Samson's story does stand as a testament that God can use our brokenness for His glory and for the advancement of His story. Our failures don't thwart God's plans. God is bigger than our mistakes. And in spite of our struggles, God isn't only willing to use us, He wants to use us.

There's a story told about the legendary founder of IBM, Thomas Watson Sr. On one occasion, a young senior executive made an error that cost IBM ten million dollars. Oops. Upon hearing the news, Watson summoned the man to his office. Upon entering, the young executive remarked, "So I'm guessing you want my resignation?" To which Watson quickly replied, "Are you kidding me? We just spent ten million dollars educating you!"[30]

Watson saw failure as education. I believe God does the same. When we blow it. When we mess up. When we struggle to the point we feel we're worthless to God. When we can't possibly imagine God wanting us on His team. When we want to call it quits, and we tender our resignation, God throws it into the recycling bin. God doesn't want our resignations. He wants our employment. He wants us with all of our struggles, with all of our blemishes, and with all of our rough edges, because He's in the business of recycling our brokenness and using it for redemptive purposes. What's more, God doesn't want our failures to remain failures. He wants our failures to become investments in learning to get things right. He wants us to learn from our mistakes, and to keep moving forward.

Not long ago, our church hosted a TobyMac concert. It was unplugged, which created space between the songs. In those spaces, Toby and the crew told stories about how they ended up together, and how many of the songs came to be. The highlight for me was hearing the background to "Get Back Up." Toby wrote the song for a friend who had absolutely blown it. And he wrote it based on what he believed God wanted his friend to hear.

The chorus goes like this:

we lose our way
we get back up again
it's never too late
to get back up again
and one day you gonna' shine again
you may be knocked down, but not out forever
we lose our way
we get back up again
so get up, get up
you gonna' shine again
it's never too late to get back up again
you may be knocked down, but not out forever

We all lose our way. We don't get things right. We struggle. We limp. We make mistakes—some bigger than others. Sometimes we fall flat on our faces. But it's in these moments we must tune our ears to the voice of God, who's saying, "Get back up. Keep moving. Regardless of what you've done, I love you. I still want you, and I can use you. Learn from your mistakes, and let's get it right." God doesn't give up on us. He wants us. And He goes out of His way to show us He loves and cares for us all.

One of the most surprising moments in the Samson story comes immediately after Samson strikes down the thousand men with the jawbone. We read, "Because he was very thirsty, he cried out to the LORD, 'You have given your servant this great victory. Must I now die of thirst and fall into the hands of the uncircumcised?' Then God opened up the hollow place in Lehi, and water came out of it.

When Samson drank, his strength returned and he revived" (Judg. 15:18–19).

It makes you wonder why God would do this. Why would He give Samson water after he's broken his vow for the umpteenth time and ruthlessly slaughtered a thousand men? The answer's simple. Because that's the kind of God He is. He gives us what we don't deserve. We don't deserve His grace, and yet He gives it. We don't deserve the relationship we can have with Him, and yet He provides it. We don't deserve the privilege of joining Him in His redemptive work in the world, and yet He invites us. And God has been doing this since the beginning of human history.

The fact that Samson shows up in Hebrews 11 is hopeful. It's hopeful because if God is willing to use someone like Samson, then God is willing to use someone like me and someone like you, with all our faults and failures. So take heart. Don't get discouraged. Whatever struggles you have—whether it's shrugging off the Spirit; harboring unforgiveness; engaging in revenge; exhibiting pride, selfishness, anger, lust, or feelings of worthlessness; or dealing with something else—know that God wants you. If you were convicted or confronted with things in the reading of this book, know that God did that in love. He loves you and He wants to help you get things right. Because God knows the healthier you are, the more joy you will have, and the more effective you will be in executing the work He's tasked you to do.

So what will it be?

What will you do with all you've seen and experienced under the sea?

How will you get right what Samson got wrong?

How will you leverage yourself for the glory of God and the good of the world?

How will you make your mark?

A Final Word of Blessing

Recorded at the end of Numbers 6, immediately following the section on the Nazirite vow, God prescribes a blessing to be spoken over the people. It's known as the Aaronic Benediction ("Aaron's Blessing"), since Aaron was initially tasked to give it. After God provides the words for the blessing (recorded in vv. 24–26), He gives its purpose by saying, "So they will put my name on the Israelites, and I will bless them" (v. 27).

As fellow human beings, created by God, receive this blessing as you seek to cultivate a healthy, dynamic, and meaningful life:

May the LORD bless you and keep you.

May the LORD make His face to shine upon you and be gracious to you.

May the LORD turn His face to you, and give you peace.

Notes

Chapter 1. Under the Sea

1. Infertility was a devastating reality for those in the ancient world, and it's a devastating reality for those today. Having experienced a second trimester miscarriage prior to having our first child, there was a period of time when my wife and I didn't know if we'd be able to have kids. It was a time of frustration, perplexity, and anxiety. And so when one learns that every barren woman in the Bible eventually has a child (or multiple children), one naturally begins to asks questions such as, "What are we doing wrong?" or "Is God punishing us in some way?" or "Are we not praying hard enough?" Let me offer a few clarifications. First, barrenness is never said to be a result of sin (Jesus addresses a similar idea in John 9:1–3). We are never given answers as to why these women were infertile. Second, in each case of these women in the Bible, God shows up to demonstrate His involvement in advancing the larger story. And third, to piggyback what was stated in the main text, every one of the boys (with the exception of the Shunnamite's son) born to these women grows up to be a very important individual in the story of Israel. Which demonstrates that God gives children to these women not only for their joy but ultimately for His greater purposes. For a more complete discussion, see K. T. Magnuson, "Childlessness," in *New Dictionary of Biblical Theology*, eds. T. Desmond Alexander, Brian S. Rosner, D. A. Carson, and Graeme Goldsworthy (Downers Grove, IL: InterVarsity Press, 2000), 404–7.
2. We don't know what became of the Shunnamite's son other than the fact that Elisha raised him from the dead (see 2 Kings 4).
3. See Judges 13:5, 7.
4. See 1 Samuel 1 and Luke 1.

5. I am most grateful to Kenneth Bailey, who in a lecture I attended shared the analogy of having views of the biblical text from the beach and from under the ocean. Little did I realize I would experience this analogy in real life, and that it would profoundly alter my way of seeing the stories in the Bible.

Chapter 2. Rushed by the Spirit

1. See James L. Crenshaw, "Samson," in *Anchor Yale Bible Dictionary* (*AYBD*), ed. David Noel Freedmen (New York: Doubleday, 1992), 5:950. See also K. Lawson Younger Jr., *The NIV Application Commentary: Judges/Ruth* (Grand Rapids, MI: Zondervan, 2002), 292.

2. The apostle John will draw upon this idea when he writes in 1 John 1:5, "This is the message we have heard from him and declare to you: God is light; in him there is no darkness at all." For a connection between God and the sun, Psalm 84:11 states, "For the LORD God is a sun and shield; the LORD bestows favor and honor; no good thing does he withhold from those whose walk is blameless."

3. Although others have contended that a name encompassing some aspect of God's personal name (*YHWH*) would have been more expected. For example, see Younger, *Judges/Ruth*, 292. Additionally, some have suggested that Samson received his name in connection to a solar cult located at the city of Beth Shemesh (literally, "House of the Sun"), located on the south side of the Sorek Valley only a couple of miles from Mahaneh Dan. For more on this, see Daniel I. Block, *The New American Commentary: Judges, Ruth* (Nashville: B&H Publishing Group, 1999), 416–17.

4. See Joshua 10:40; Judges 1:9; Obadiah 1:19; and Zechariah 7:7.

5. "פַּעַם" (*pa'am*), Ludwig Koehler and Walter Baumgartner, *The Hebrew and Aramaic Lexicon of the OT* (*HALOT*) (New York: Brill Academic Publishing, 1994), 3:952.

6. Paul H. Wright, *Rose Then and Now Bible Map Atlas with Biblical Background and Culture* (Torrance, CA: Rose Publishing, 2012), 43.

7. See Numbers 6:9–12.

8. The eating of anything unclean is addressed in the conversation with Manoah's wife and the angel of the LORD in Judges 13:4, 7.

9. See Leviticus 5:2–3, Leviticus 11, and Deuteronomy 14 for regulations on clean and unclean.

10. "מִשְׁתֶּה" (*mishteh*), *HALOT*, 2:653.

11. Most translations use "foxes" here. However, the Hebrew word for "fox" is *shu'al*. *Shu'al* is a generic term that can also refer to a "jackal." Both foxes and jackals were native to the land at this time. Since foxes are solitary animals and jackals are found in packs, it is more likely Samson utilizes the jackals as his means for destruction. See Daniel I. Block, *Zondervan Illustrated Bible Backgrounds Commentary: Old Testament (ZIBBCOT)*, ed. John H. Walton (Grand Rapids, MI: Zondervan, 2009), 2:197.

12. The story is seething with irony here. Samson kills these Philistines with a jawbone he finds in an area identified as "Lehi," which in Hebrew means "jawbone."

13. We don't know for certain if Samson retires. However, as we'll discuss later in Chapter 6, Samson is the only judge to have his length of reign recorded both during his life and after his death. For every other judge whose length of reign is recorded in Judges, it is mentioned immediately after his death. Also, I am specifically using the language of "retires" because it signifies to us that Samson quit his job. Retirement is a modern phenomenon and not a biblical one. People didn't retire in the biblical period. Generally speaking, their job ended when they died.

14. See Block, *ZIBBCOT*, 2:200.

15. Some offer an alternative reading for Judges 16:3 by suggesting Samson headed off on the path to Hebron and dumped the gates on a hill after leaving Gaza. See John H. Walton, Victor H. Matthews, and Mark W. Chavalas, *The IVP Bible Background Commentary: Old Testament* (Downers Grove, IL: InterVarsity Press, 2000), 268–69.

16. Ibid., 270.

17. Notably, a Philistine temple from the time of Samson was found in the archaeological excavations at Tell Qasile, a site located within the modern Israeli city of Tel Aviv. Although on a smaller scale than what the temple of Gaza would have been, the design reveals two central stone pillar bases, less than ten feet apart, where tall wooden pillars would have been set to support the center axis of a long room design. For more information on the temple, or to see an isometric reconstruction of a temple of Dagon at Beth Shean, see Block, *ZIBB-COT*, 2:203.

18. Lois Tverberg, *Walking in the Dust of Rabbi Jesus* (Grand Rapids, MI: Zondervan, 2012), 36–37.

19. "צָלַח" (*tzalach*), Francis Brown, S. R. Driver, and Charles A. Briggs, *The Brown-Driver-Briggs Hebrew and English Lexicon* (*BDB*) (Peabody, MA: Hendrickson Publishers, 1994), 852; and *The New International Dictionary of Old Testament Theology & Exegesis* (*NIDOTTE*), ed. Willem A. VanGemeren (Grand Rapids, MI: Zondervan, 1997), 3:804.

20. *YHWH* (often spelled "Yahweh") is the intimate, personal, covenantal name of God first given by God to Moses in Exodus 3.

21. See Judges 3:10, 14:6, 19, 15:14, 1 Samuel 10:6, Isaiah 11:2, Ezekiel 11:5, and 2 Chronicles 20:14.

22. (Note: This is a more technical note for those of you who understand the Hebrew language—or are interested in it—to provide additional context for understanding the Spirit of the LORD's activity in the Samson narrative.) I just stated that the specific Hebrew phrase used in connection with *tzalach* in this passage—*alav ruach YHWH* (literally, "upon him the Spirit of the LORD")—shows up only eight times in the Bible (and I listed those references above). The entire phrase, which includes *tzalach*, used in the Samson narrative is *vatitzlach alav ruach YHWH* (literally, "and it rushed upon him the Spirit of the LORD"). This phrase shows up only four times in the Bible, three of which are in the Samson narrative (Judges 14:6, 14:19, 15:14). The only other place this exact phrase shows up is in 1 Samuel 10:6, which reads, "Then the Spirit of the LORD will rush upon you, and you will prophesy with them and be turned into another man" (ESV). The meaning of this passage is difficult to understand, particularly the phrase "and be turned into another man." What makes it even more challenging is how the passage comes to fruition four verses later. 1 Samuel 10:10 reads, "When they came to Gibeah, behold, a group of prophets met him, and the Spirit of God rushed upon him, and he prophesied among them" (ESV). Notice the phrase the "Spirit of the LORD [*YHWH*]" in verse 6 switches to the "Spirit of God [*Elohim*]" in verse 10. This switch changes how we view these passages alongside the Judges passages because once it becomes a different phrase in verse 10, a different meaning is being communicated, and therefore, it doesn't help us make sense of what's happening in the Samson account. Thus, we don't have any other passages or precedents for understanding the language used in connection with the phrase *vatit-*

zlach alav ruach YHWH in the Samson narrative. We have to look at it based on its context in the story to surmise what's happening.

23. At times, based on a Hebrew verb's construction or the context of the passage, translators must supply phrases such as "so that" to accurately present what's being stated in the original language. However, in other cases, the supplying of such phrases is an interpretive decision. The "so that" in connection to the Spirit's rushing is interpretive because the verb construction of *tzalach* and the context of the passage do not demand it.

24. Which, again, is how the New Revised Standard Version has translated this passage.

25. See 1 Kings 20:35–36.

26. See Jeremiah 5:5–6.

Chapter 3. Seventy-Seven Times

1. "שָׂנֵא" (*sānē*), *NIDOTTE*, 3:1256–59.

2. Oxford Dictionary Online. Accessed September 4, 2013, http://oxforddictionaries.com/us/definition/american_english/revenge?q=revenge.

3. "נקה" (*naqah*), *HALOT*, 2:720.

4. Depending upon the context, "Torah" can be used to denote the entire Hebrew Scriptures (Old Testament) or, in this case, the first five books of the Bible (Genesis, Exodus, Leviticus, Numbers, and Deuteronomy).

5. See also Leviticus 24:20 and Deuteronomy 19:21.

6. In addition to *lex talionis*, God also designated six cities to serve as "cities of refuge" (where someone who accidentally killed another could take refuge) in order to prevent revenge killings from being exacted. See Deuteronomy 19:1–14.

7. There is considerable debate as to whether an injury was to be repaid literally (i.e., a literal eye for an eye) or whether an individual was to be repaid monetarily. For helpful discussions on varying views, see Nahum M. Sarna, *The JPS Torah Commentary: Exodus* (Philadelphia: Jewish Publication Society, 1991), 125–27, and H. B. Huffmon, "Lex Talionis," in *AYBD*, 4:321–22.

8. I've modified this sentence of the translation to reflect our discussion from Chapter 2.

9. Notably, when Samson calls on God for help, he uses three different names for God in the original Hebrew—*Adonai* (Lord), *YHWH* (God's personal name), and *Elohim* (God). It appears he's trying everything he can to curry favor and coax God into doing what he wants.

10. Samson killed thirty men for losing a bet. With the loss of his wife and father-in-law (which probably wasn't that big of a loss to Samson owing to his recent antics), I have to believe he killed more than thirty in his fit of rage. If he did, this would obviously bode well for the escalating numbers. However, we'll never know. Why we aren't given the number of deaths in this incident is a mystery.

11. See entry "ἐκδικέω" (*ekdikeō*) in *A Greek-English Lexicon of the New Testament and Other Early Christian Literature, 3rd Edition* (*BDAG*), ed. Frederick William Danker (Chicago: University of Chicago Press, 2001), 300–301.

12. When Paul quotes God as saying, "It is mine to avenge; I will repay," this is coming from Deuteronomy 32:35.

13. Perhaps Paul also has Psalm 37:8 ("Refrain from anger and turn from wrath; do not fret—it leads only to evil.") in mind when he's composing this letter.

14. A brilliant insight I gleaned from Rob Bell in his NOOMA film, *007 Luggage* (Grand Rapids, MI: Flannel, 2005), DVD.

15. Contrary to some popular interpretations, Jesus is not advocating for pacifism here. He's advocating for nonviolence, which actively confronts a broken situation, but never does so with violence. For a brilliant exposition on what Jesus is doing here, see Walter Wink, *The Powers That Be: Theology for a New Millennium* (New York: Doubleday, 1998), 98–111.

16. This quote is from the Babylonian Talmud (*b. Yoma* 86b, 87a) and comes in the context of the rabbis being concerned about the unrepentant nature of an individual who continues to repeat the same offense.

17. By the way, every time you quote a movie line in a conversation, you're engaging in remez. So if someone asks for the truth, and you shout back at them, "You can't handle the truth!" you're actually utilizing a biblical teaching method. However, use sparingly. When the other party doesn't see it coming, it can be a bit unnerving.

18. Michael J. Wilkins, *Zondervan Illustrated Bible Backgrounds Commentary: New Testament* (*ZIBBCNT*), ed. Clinton E. Arnold (Grand Rapids, MI: Zondervan, 2002), 1:115.

19. Klyne Snodgrass, *Stories with Intent: A Comprehensive Guide to the Parables of Jesus* (Grand Rapids, MI: Wm. B. Eerdmans Publishing Co., 2008), 66.

20. Wilkins, *ZIBBCNT*, 1:116.

21. Information was gathered from the International Forgiveness Institute website. Accessed on April 8, 2013, http://www.internationalforgiveness .com/about-us/team.

22. As quoted in Stephen Post and Jill Neimark, *Why Good Things Happen to Good People* (New York: Broadway Books, 2007), 81.

23. I am greatly indebted to many people who over the years have taught me volumes on forgiveness, but I specifically want to acknowledge the fine work of Catherine Clair Larson, who brilliantly condensed the overarching research that has been done in the area of forgiveness and presented a compelling case for how we go about understanding forgiveness. Because of the impact of her work, a good portion of the structure and content of what follows is based on what I learned in *As We Forgive: Stories of Reconciliation from Rwanda* (Grand Rapids, MI: Zondervan, 2009).

24. "ἀφίημι" (*aphiēmi*), *BDAG*, 156–57.

25. Anne Lamott, *Traveling Mercies: Some Thoughts on Faith* (New York: Random House, 1999), 134.

26. "נָשָׂא" (*nasa*), *BDB*, 669.

27. *Ed's Story: Film 5—Ask Forgiveness* (Grand Rapids, MI: Flannel, 2012), DVD.

28. Larson, *As We Forgive*, 122.

29. Ibid., 264.

Chapter 4. Scuffed Knees

1. "גָּאוֹן" (*ga'on*), *NIDOTTE*, 1:789.

2. "שֶׁבֶר" (*shever*), *BDB*, 991.

3. The number fifty-five hundred comes from five governors each giving eleven hundred shekels (see Judges 16:5). The textual evidence for the five governors (or "rulers") of the five main cities of the Philistines is found in Joshua 13:3. The governors are again referenced in Judges 3:3. Also, a "shekel" at this time was not a coin but a unit of weight. Coinage would not be invented until the seventh century BC.

4. Block, *ZIBBCOT*, 2:200.

5. I gleaned this insight from Michael Wilcock, *The Message of Judges* (Downers Grove, IL: InterVarsity Press, 1992), 130.

6. "Delilah," *AYBD*, 2:133.

7. The Hebrew language is rich. Words can have numerous meanings, and this is the case when it comes to the meaning of "Delilah." There are several meanings that keep surfacing in the scholarly literature, and all of them are helpful in understanding this peculiar relationship between Samson and Delilah. In addition to "of the night," Delilah's name can mean "long hair," "slight" (as in a slight or slender body type), as well as "flirtatious." So the showdown is between night versus light, long hair versus long hair, slight versus might, and flirtatious versus womanizer. See the entry "Samson" in *NIDOTTE*, 4:1167, and "Delilah" in *AYBD*, 2:133, for the various meanings of Delilah's name.

8. Relatively speaking in light of Samson's prior behavior.

9. This idiom in connection with Samson is found in Wright's brilliant book, *Rose Then and Now Bible Map Atlas with Biblical Background and Culture*, 45.

10. Block, *ZIBBCOT*, 2:200–1.

11. This isn't the first time Samson has fallen prey to a severe case of nagging (see Judges 14:16–17).

12. What's fascinating is the media will often employ the language of "The Fall of So-and-So." Where does this language come from? Proverbs.

13. Jeff Cook, *Seven: The Deadly Sins and the Beatitudes* (Grand Rapids, MI: Zondervan, 2008), 33.

14. Sadly, another reason people won't openly share their addictions is because they believe if they are given enough time, they will be able to conquer their issues alone. Here's the problem: You can't do it alone. And the greatest lie the evil one whispers into our vulnerable little ears is this: "You can do it. Nobody has to know. You have the power to overcome this. Keep trying. Just give it enough time." It's a lie from the pit of hell, and if you're struggling and you've accepted this lie, the fact you are still addicted exposes the lie for what it is. Please drop your pride and get help.

15. "σωφρονέω" (*sōphroneō*), *BDAG*, 986.

16. "ταπεινόω" (*tapeinoō*), *BDAG*, 990. Switching now from Greek to Hebrew, what's fascinating is that the Hebrew word for "humility" is *shephel*. Samson lives in the "Shephelah," a region that serves as a buffer between the coastal plain to the west and the high hills of Judah to the east. Shephelah derives its name from *shephel* because the rolling

hills of the Shephelah are low and humble before the hills of the high country. The irony here is that Samson lives in "Humbleville" and yet he is anything but humble.

17. Dwight A. Pryor, *A Continuing Quest* (Dayton: Center for Judaic Christian Studies, 2011), 95.

18. Ibid., 96.

19. Ibid.

20. Ray Vander Laan once shared with me that a helpful way of both acknowledging praise someone is offering you and deflecting it to God is simply to respond with the words "Bless God." For example, if someone approaches you and compliments you in some way, responding with, "Thank you," is a subtle way of acknowledging their compliment and taking the credit for yourself (again, it's subtle, but it's there). However, when you respond with, "Bless God," you are both acknowledging their praise as well as indicating that the source of your ability is God, and it is God who is to be ultimately praised for whatever good and helpful aspects came out of what they value in you.

21. In addition to defining *barakh* as "to praise" and "to bless," most Hebrew lexicons will also define *barakh* as "to kneel." In Hebrew, words that share the same consonantal root (there are no vowels in Hebrew) are related in meaning. A word that shares the same root as *barakh* is *berekh* (both contain "b-r-kh"), which means "knee." Hence, another way of saying "to kneel" is "to bend a knee." See the entry on *barakh* ("ברך") in *HALOT*, 1:159–60.

22. I am most grateful to George DeJong, a dear friend and mentor, who originally pointed out to me the meaning of *barakh* and made several connections that shaped this section of the chapter. Check out what this man is up to at www.UnderTheFigTree.org.

23. See also Matthew 20:28.

24. For a fantastic discussion on the father-son relationship between a rabbi and his disciples, hunt down David Bivin's *New Light on the Difficult Words of Jesus* (Holland, MI: En-Gedi Resource Center, 2005), 19–20.

25. See Craig S. Keener, *The IVP Bible Background Commentary: New Testament* (Downers Grove, IL: InterVarsity Press, 1993), 296–97, as well as Andreas J. Köstenberger, *ZIBBCNT*, 2:131.

26. See Mark 10:42–44 and Luke 22:25–26.

27. *Ga'on*, the word for "pride," is also the same Hebrew word for "majesty"—as in God's majesty. So perhaps we could say that pride is when we mistake God's majesty as our own. Just a thought.

Chapter 5. Designed for Struggle

1. As quoted in Kenneth Bailey, *Paul Through Mediterranean Eyes: Cultural Studies in 1 Corinthians* (Downers Grove, IL: InterVarsity Press, 2011), 344.
2. For a helpful discussion on the thirty men, see Block, *Judges, Ruth*, 431–32.
3. I first heard the concepts behind "helper suitable" in a Torah class my good friend George DeJong was leading. After being enamored of its implications, George and I spent significant time further developing this. So I am greatly indebted to George for his work and assistance on this topic.
4. "עֵזֶר" (*ezer*), *NIDOTTE*, 3:378–79.
5. A classic example is Psalm 121, which begins, "I lift up my eyes to the mountains—where does my help (*ezer*) come from? My help (*ezer*) comes from the LORD, the Maker of heaven and earth" (vv.1–2). I encourage you to read the rest of the Psalm (it's only eight verses) to see other ways God serves the people as an *ezer*.
6. "נֶגֶר" (*neged*), *HALOT*, 2:666–67.
7. If you would like to learn more on the topic of Nonviolent Communication (NVC), check out Marshall B. Rosenberg, *Nonviolent Communication: A Language of Life* (Encinitas, CA: PuddleDancer Press, 2003).

Chapter 6. Gotta Have Blue Eyes

1. "נָזַר" (*nazar*), *BDB*, 634.
2. See Numbers 6:7.
3. "נֶזֶר" (*nezer*), *BDB*, 634.
4. See Numbers 6:9–12. In this passage, the shaving of one's head comes in connection to encountering the death of someone or something. However, there is a consensus that any violation of the Nazirite restrictions should result in the shaving of one's head.
5. Israel had fallen prey to this as they neared the end of their wilderness journeying, and it resulted in the death of 24,000 Israelites. See Numbers 25.

6. This is in part why the story of the prodigal son in Luke 15 is so electric. It wasn't just that he wanted his inheritance, thereby smiting his father, but that he also offended the entire community.

7. Circumcision was the sign of the covenantal relationship between God and his people (see Genesis 17). When Samson's parents use the language of "uncircumcised Philistines," they are highlighting the fact the Philistines are not part of the covenantal people of God, and thus off-limits for marriage to an Israelite (again, per Deuteronomy 7).

8. The last part of Samson's prayer is tricky to translate from the Hebrew. Protestant translations have "for my two eyes." However, Jewish translations—such as the JPS (Jewish Publication Society) and the Complete Jewish Bible—render it "for one of my two eyes." When there is confusion, I generally lean in the direction of the Jewish translations.

9. Interestingly, according to Moses' instructions, it was never God's intention to have a single judge ruling the land. In Deuteronomy 16:18, we read, "Appoint judges and officials for each of your tribes in every town the LORD your God is giving you, and they shall judge the people fairly." The system we see playing out in the book of Judges was flawed from the start.

10. See 1 Kings 2:10–11.

11. See Judges 13:2.

12. Read Judges 17 and 18 to get the background information on Micah and this idol.

13. The tabernacle was a large tent structure (see Exodus 25–40) where God localized His presence on earth. And the place of the tabernacle was where the Israelites were to worship God. Worshipping idols or engaging in formal worship anywhere other than at the location of the tabernacle (and later, the temple) was strictly prohibited.

14. For those of you keen on dates, the "time of the captivity of the land" (referenced in Judges 18:30) begins in 734 BC when Tigleath-Pilesar III, ruler of Assyria, attacks the Northern Kingdom of Israel.

15. I patterned this succinct summary after something I heard Kent Dobson do in a teaching entitled "Samson's Faith" (taught at Mars Hill Bible Church on July 29, 2012). So much thanks to Kent for helping me frame these brief summary statements.

16. See Judges 18:1 and 19:1.

17. Remember that Samson's decisions led to his wife and father-in-law being burned to death.

18. The three passages that make up the "Shema" are Deuteronomy 6:4–9, Deuteronomy 11:13–21; and Numbers 15:37–41. *Shema* is a Hebrew word meaning "hear," and the prayer gets its name from the first word of Deuteronomy 6:4, which begins, "Hear O Israel…" As stated in the main text, the Shema is recited every morning and every evening. However, in modern Judaism, the third section (Numbers 15:37–41) is only recited in the morning when the *tallit*, a present-day representation of the ancient garments, which encompasses the tassels, is put on.

19. In Hebrew, "Red Sea" is *Yam Suf*—literally the "Reed Sea" or "Sea of Reeds."

20. See Exodus 3:12.

21. I'm grateful for the work Rob Bell and Don Golden did on the functionality of ancient priests in their book, *Jesus Wants to Save Christians: A Manifesto for the Church in Exile* (Grand Rapids, MI: Zondervan, 2008), 30–31. Understanding the functionality of a priest in the ancient world and what God was then calling His followers to be and do was a monumental moment in my life as a Christian. It changed my understanding of what a Christian is to look like in the world and what purpose the church must serve if it is going to reflect the heart of God and actually be a compelling force for good in the world.

22. Marshall McLuhan, *Understanding Media: The Extensions of Man* (New York: McGraw-Hill, 1964).

23. "The Medium Is the Message." Dictionary.com. Accessed on January 29, 2013, http://dictionary.reference.com/browse/the medium is the message.

24. Some of you may be wondering about how this identity of a "kingdom of priests" conflicted with the role of the Levites, who were specifically set apart by God to be priests within the Children of Israel. Whereas the Levites were commissioned to serve as a direct intermediary between the Israelites and God, the Israelites as a whole were to mediate between the world and God.

25. Many thanks to Chuck Swanson for coming up with this great metaphor.

26. See Chapters 2–9 in the New Testament book of Hebrews.

Chapter 7. Give Us What You've Got

1. It's interesting that Samson will only "begin" to deliver Israel from the hands of the Philistines, rather than "completely" deliver them. According to some, this points to the incompleteness of Samson's life's work. See Arthur E. Cundall and Leon Morris, *Judges and Ruth* (Downers Grove, IL: InterVarsity Press, 2008), 152.

2. There are two main possibilities for dating the Exodus, which gives us an idea of when Israel entered into the land of Canaan (i.e., forty years after the Exodus date). The early date for the Exodus is 1445 BC. The later date for the Exodus is 1250 BC.

3. For information on the migration of the Sea Peoples and the Philistines, see Wright, *Rose Then and Now Bible Map Atlas*, 42–43, and Block, *ZIBBCOT*, 2:120–22.

4. David Gilman Romano, *The Olympic Games: How They All Began* (Biblical Archaeology Society, 2008), 28–29. PDF e-book. Available at http://www.biblicalarchaeology.org/free-ebooks/the-olympic-games-how-they-all-began.

5. An insightful observation I first came across in Younger, *Judges/Ruth*, 316–17.

6. We know the Philistines had at least enough appreciation for Samson's abilities so as not to abuse or destroy his corpse following the temple's collapse. They allowed Samson's family to take his body and bury it in Manoah's tomb, between Zorah and Eshtaol (see Judges 16:31).

7. For the Israelite culture, nudity was shameful—both for the viewer and the one exposed.

8. Sadly, Dwight Pryor's life ended prematurely, owing to disease. If you're not familiar with this incredible man or his outstanding work, please visit www.jcstudies.com.

9. Luke does give us a story of Jesus when he's twelve, and he's at the temple debating with the religious teachers (see Luke 2:41–52).

10. See Genesis 1:27 and Psalm 8:5.

11. Steven Pressfield, *The War of Art: Break Through the Blocks and Win Your Inner Creative Battles* (New York: Grand Central Publishing, 2002), 146.

12. For a more comprehensive approach, I'd highly recommend Jon Acuff's phenomenal book *Start: Punch Fear in the Face, Escape Average and Do Work That Matters* (Nashville: Thomas Nelson, 2013).

13. This is a new question I've added to the repertoire after hearing Troy Evans, lead pastor of the EDGE Urban Fellowship (Grand Rapids, MI), speak at the 2013 TEDxMacatawa conference here in Holland, MI. He made the insightful observation that our greatest passion may actually be connected to our greatest hurt. That out of the pain we experienced in the past comes a passion to help others who are going through what we went through.

14. John Piper, *When I Don't Desire God: How to Fight for Joy* (Wheaton, IL: Crossway, 2004), 13.

Chapter 8. Hope for Faulty People

1. Gideon's story is found in Judges 6–8.
2. Barak and Deborah's stories are found in Judges 4–5.
3. There is a popular opinion that Jephthah did not go through with the sacrifice of his daughter. However, this is a very late tradition, begun in the medieval period. The biblical witness is that he sacrificed his daughter as a burnt offering (see Judges 11:39). Jephthah's story is found in Judges 10:6–11:40.
4. Genesis 3:6.
5. Genesis 4:8.
6. Genesis 9:20–21.
7. Genesis 16:1–4.
8. Genesis 12:10–16; Genesis 20:1–2.
9. Genesis 18:15.
10. Genesis 26:7.
11. Genesis 27.
12. Genesis 29–30.
13. Genesis 37:5–11.
14. Genesis 38.
15. Exodus 2:11–12.
16. Exodus 3–4.
17. Numbers 20:1–13.
18. Exodus 32.
19. Joshua 6:17.
20. 2 Samuel 11. Some contend that David's initial encounter with Bathsheba wasn't adultery but rape.
21. 1 Kings 2:1–12.
22. 1 Kings 11:1–6.

23. 1 Kings 19.
24. Jeremiah 1:4–6.
25. Luke 7:18–20.
26. Luke 9:43–48.
27. Matthew 26:31–35, 69–75.
28. Acts 7:59–8:3.
29. Younger, *Judges/Ruth*, 302.
30. Stefan H. Thomke, *Experimentation Matters: Unlocking the Potential of New Technologies for Innovation* (Boston: Harvard Business Review Press, 2003), 214.

Acknowledgments

Many thanks go to:

Jana Burson, for believing in this project from day one and for pushing me to be a better writer. You're a fabulous editor, and now a friend. Thank you for everything.

Laura Wheeler, for being a resourceful editorial assistant and for helping with all the nuts and bolts.

Tareth Mitch, for masterfully stewarding this book to the finish line.

All the other amazing people at FaithWords and Hachette, for giving me a shot and for making this project such a wonderful experience. It's been an honor working with you.

Brad Nelson, for walking with me in ways I can't even begin to thank you for. This book is infinitely better because of your feedback and assistance.

Chris Ferebee, for taking me on and representing me well. You're a brilliant agent, and I'm grateful for our friendship.

John Topliff, for passionately insisting at JP's that I begin writing now.

Rob Bell, for getting the ball rolling and for providing insightful feedback.

Travis West, for helping me keep my Hebrew straight. If I made any errors, it's my fault and not yours.

Larry Largent, for saving the day and helping me clarify a couple of key sections.

My grandpa (Jack Gray), Matt Engle, Ben and Stacie Post, and Corey and Amanda Becker, for reading a draft along the way and providing helpful feedback.

My extended family, for encouraging me to pursue this life of teaching and for being a constant source of love and support.

Denyon, Aryah, and Calyx, for being the joys of my life and for coming downstairs in the mornings to give me hugs while I wrote. I couldn't wait for my door to open.

Shallon, for being with me every step of this writing journey and in our eleven years of marriage. There aren't words to convey my love and appreciation. Looking forward to the next eleven.